Coloring Octangles

An absorbing and fascinating coloring experience

Chandra Davis, ATR~BC, LCPC

Introduction

It's possible you are entirely new to the concept of using art to heal. So today, I'm going to give you a quick overview of how this all works.

First of all let's talk about the most common question I hear...
"Do I need to have a background or talent for art to do this?"

The answer is easy: No!

You see... the power of art making is not only about how beautifully you create your artwork, or even what the end result is. It's also about the PROCESS of creating the art as an expression of how you are feeling about a particular issue you're dealing with.

For example, if I said, "What color makes you happy?" You might have an instant picture in your head of what that color looks like.

Think about that for just a minute.

There's no right or wrong answer--it's just whatever happens naturally for you.

The same principle can be applied to coloring. You begin with a template illustration, and from that template, you can create a variety of artwork based on your personalized color palette.

In a nutshell, that's the beginning of how art therapy works!

It's proven that the artistic expression of your ideas, emotions, and thoughts can result in a reduction of stress, increased creativity, and more peace of mind. It can be pretty awesome when you realize how powerful it is!

Remember, there's no right or wrong in this--all you have to do is trust the process.

And after years of working with clients, I realized how much this could help people who don't have the time, money, or resources to experience art therapy in a clinical setting.

So I created Art Therapy Lab, a series of self-paced tools and resources available for people of all ages and skill levels to experience the benefits of art therapy.

I sincerely believe you may find this to be extremely helpful. I hope you'll take advantage of this to support you in creating a healthier, happier life for yourself.

To your health and healing,
Chandra Davis, ATR-BC, LCPC

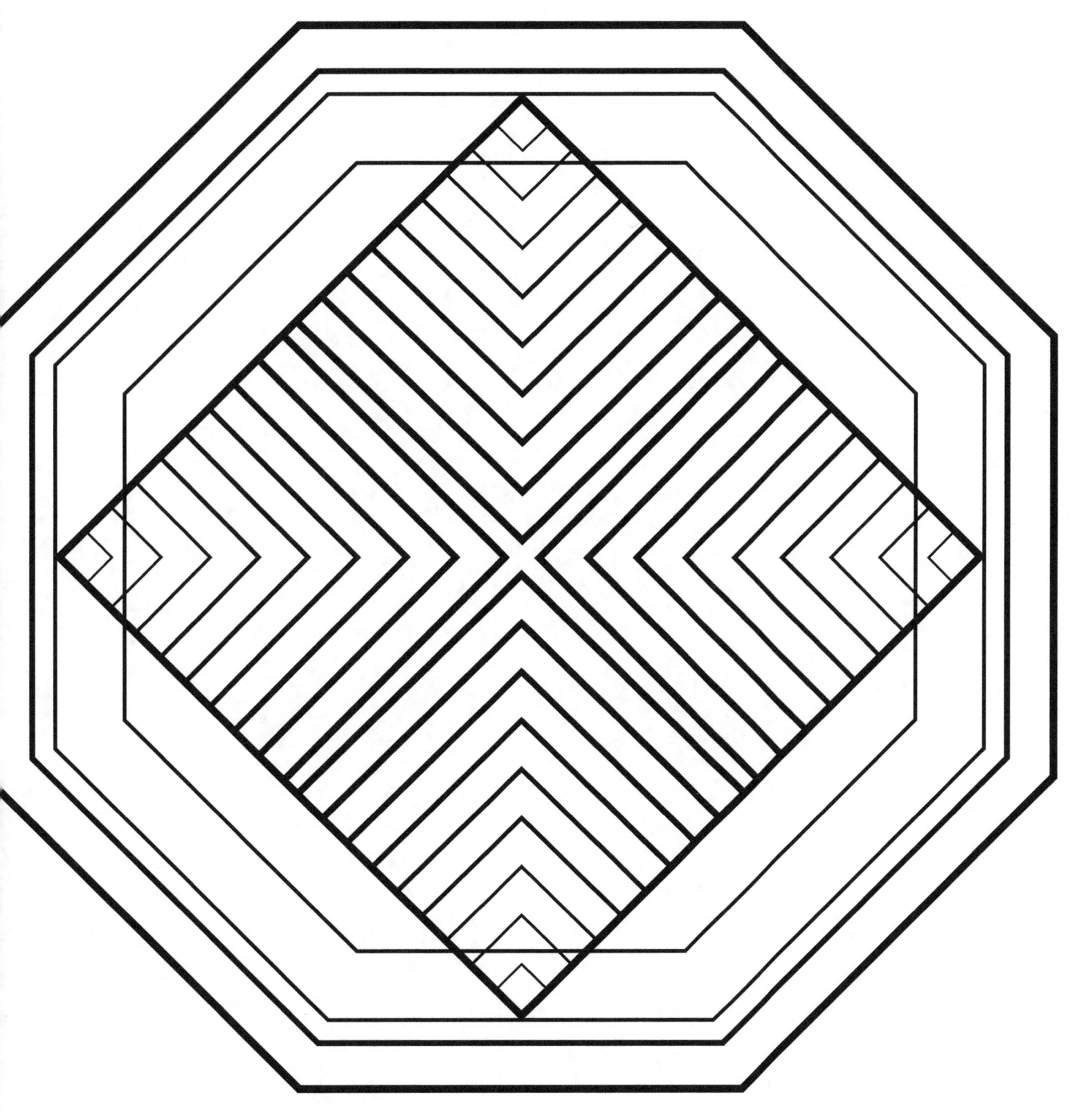

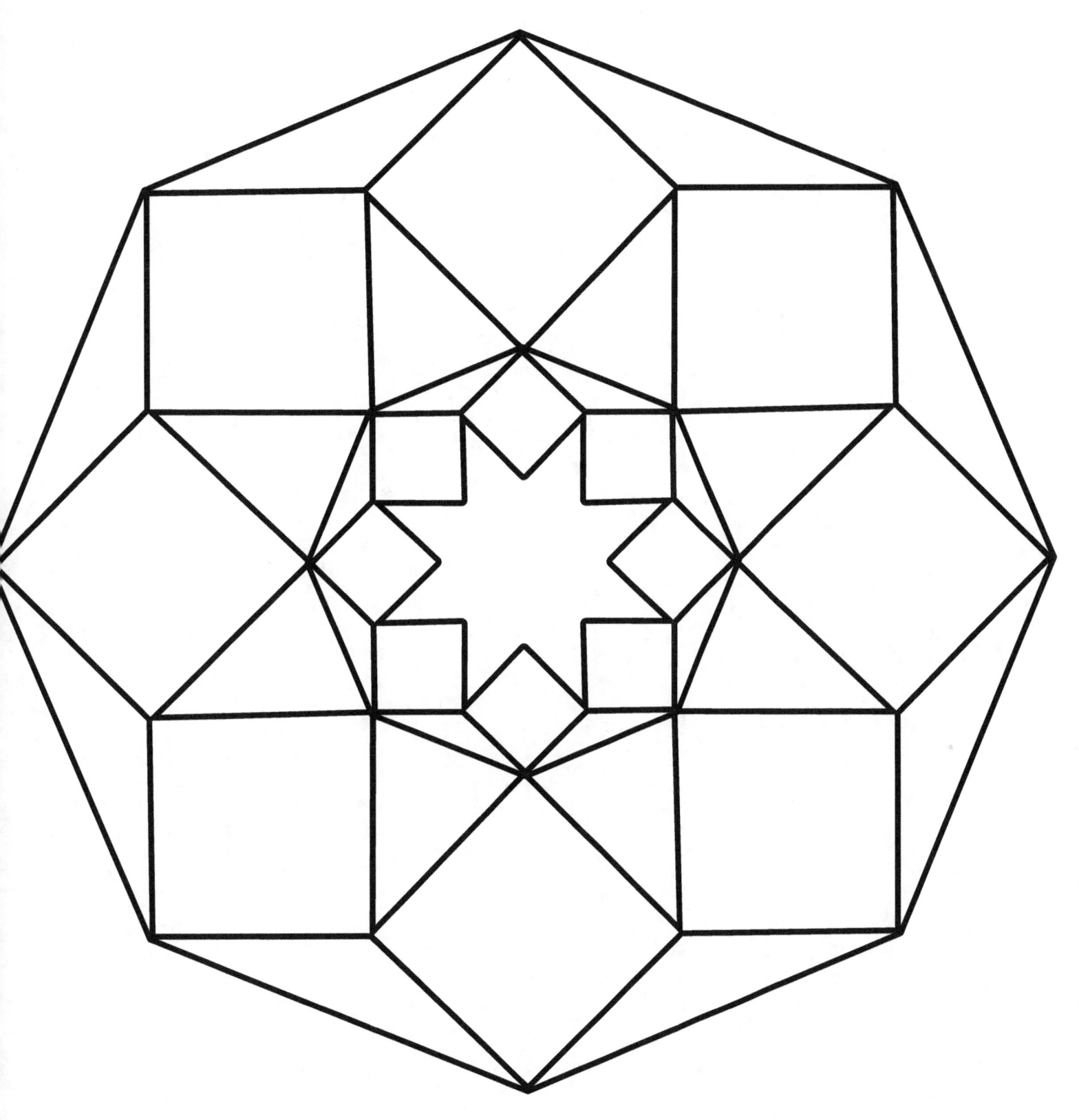

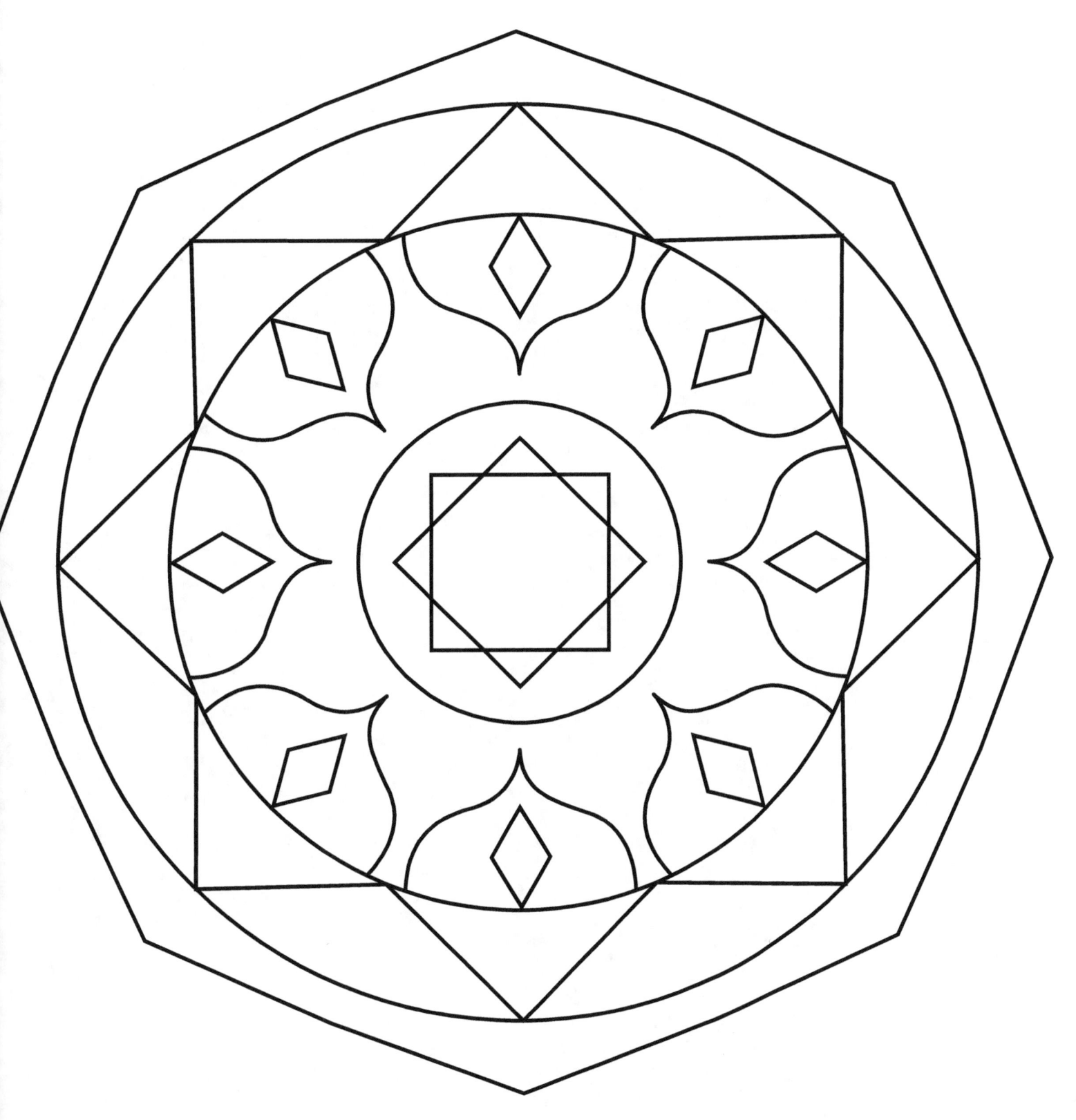

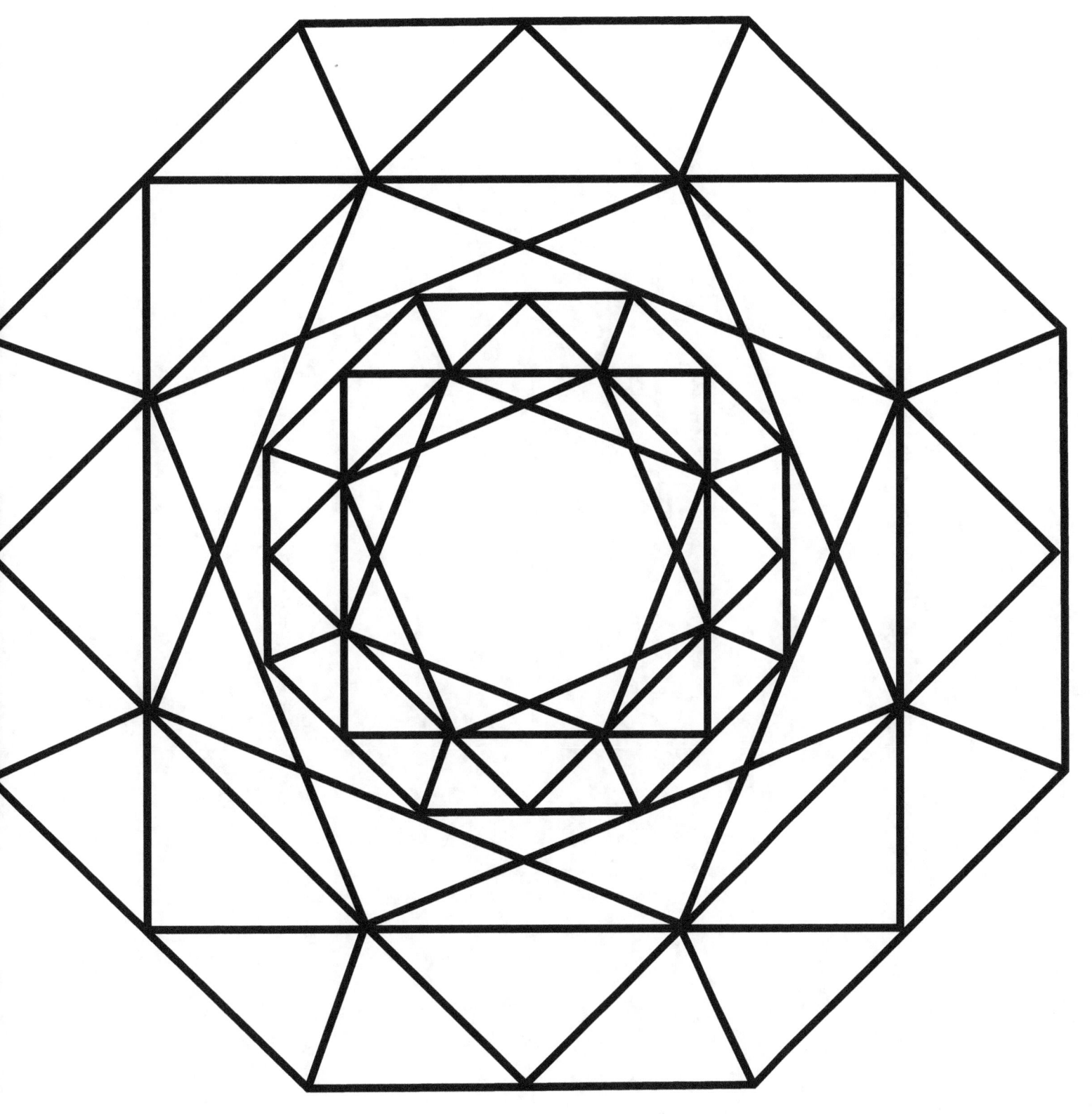

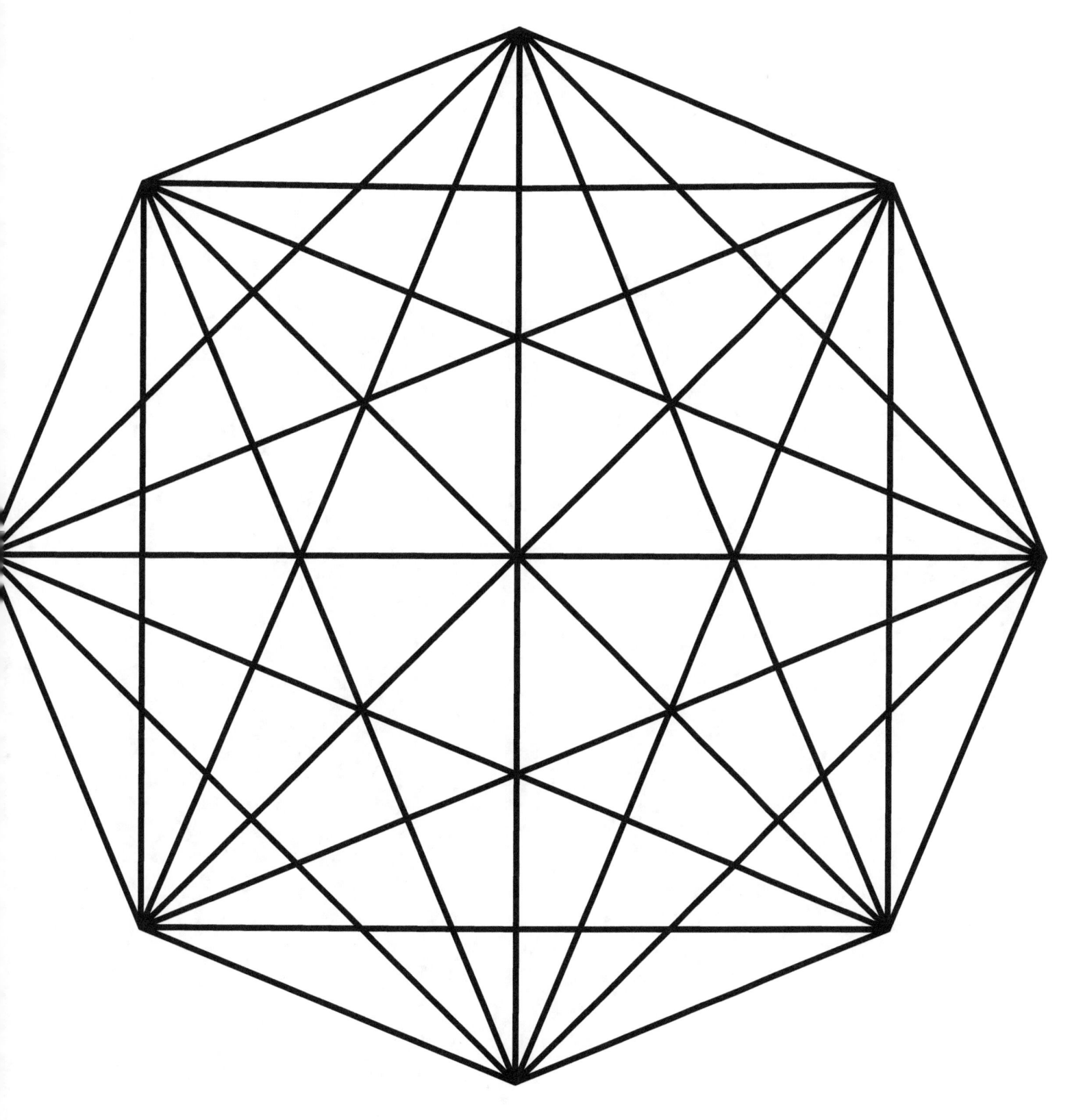

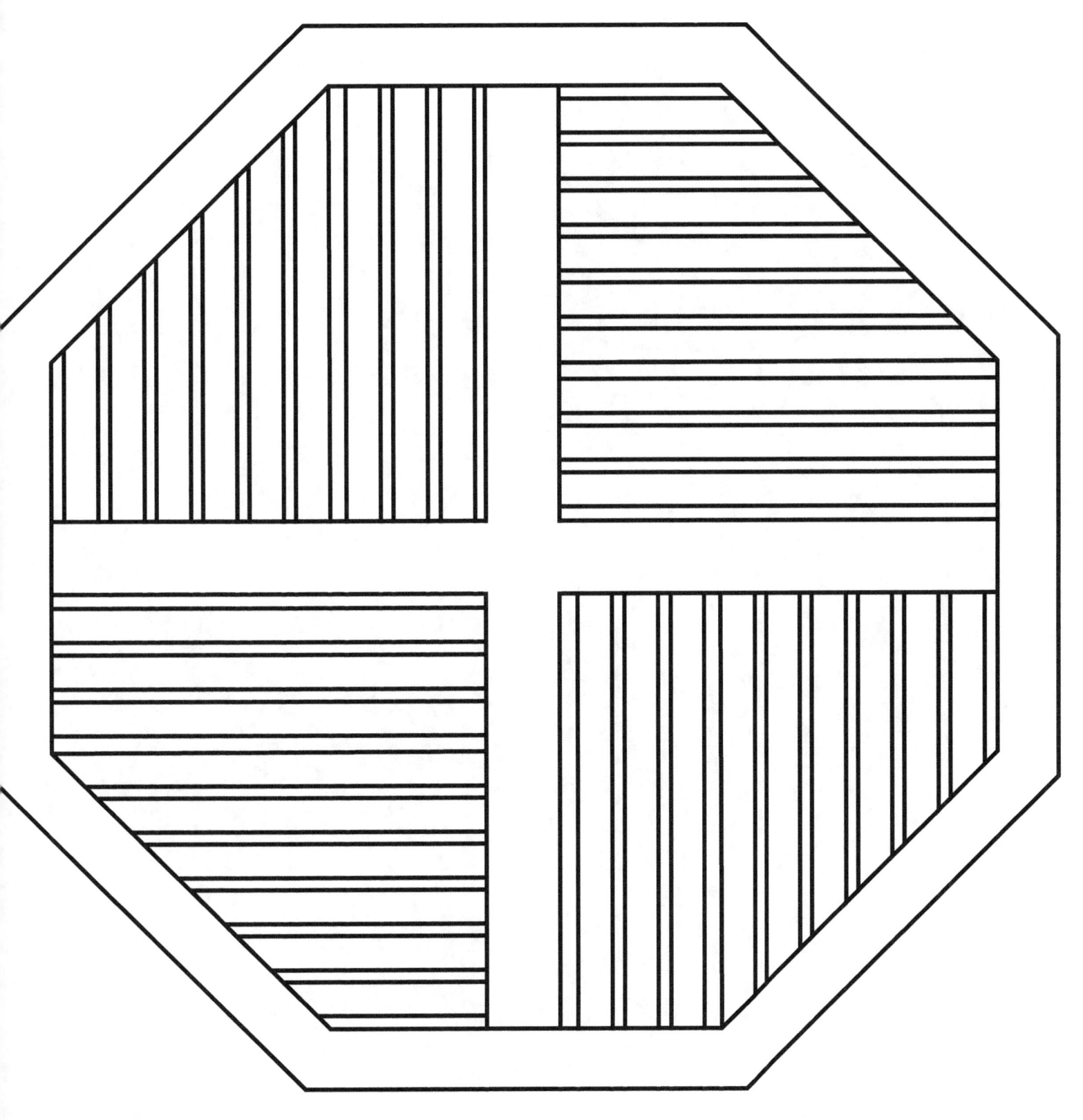

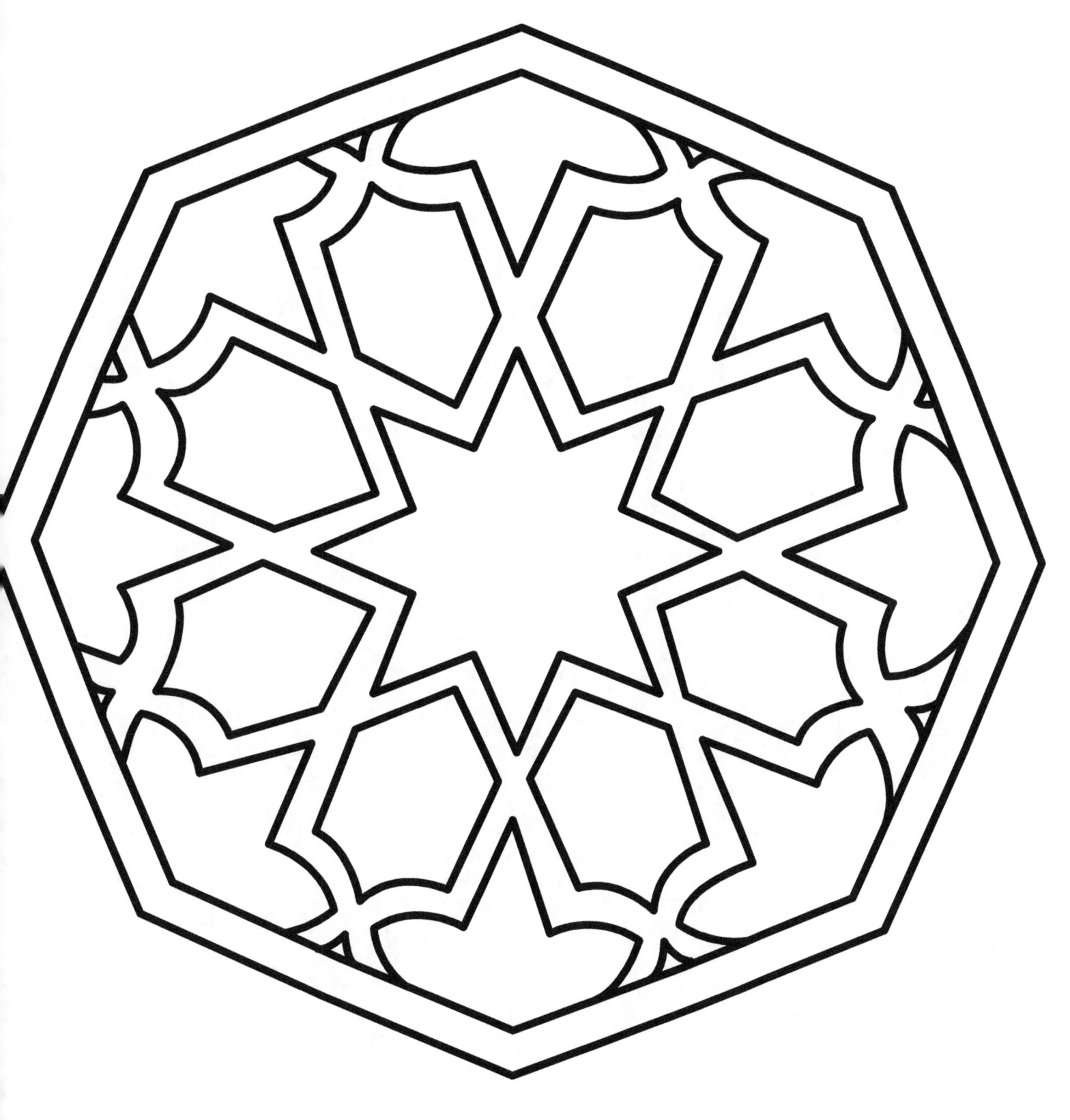

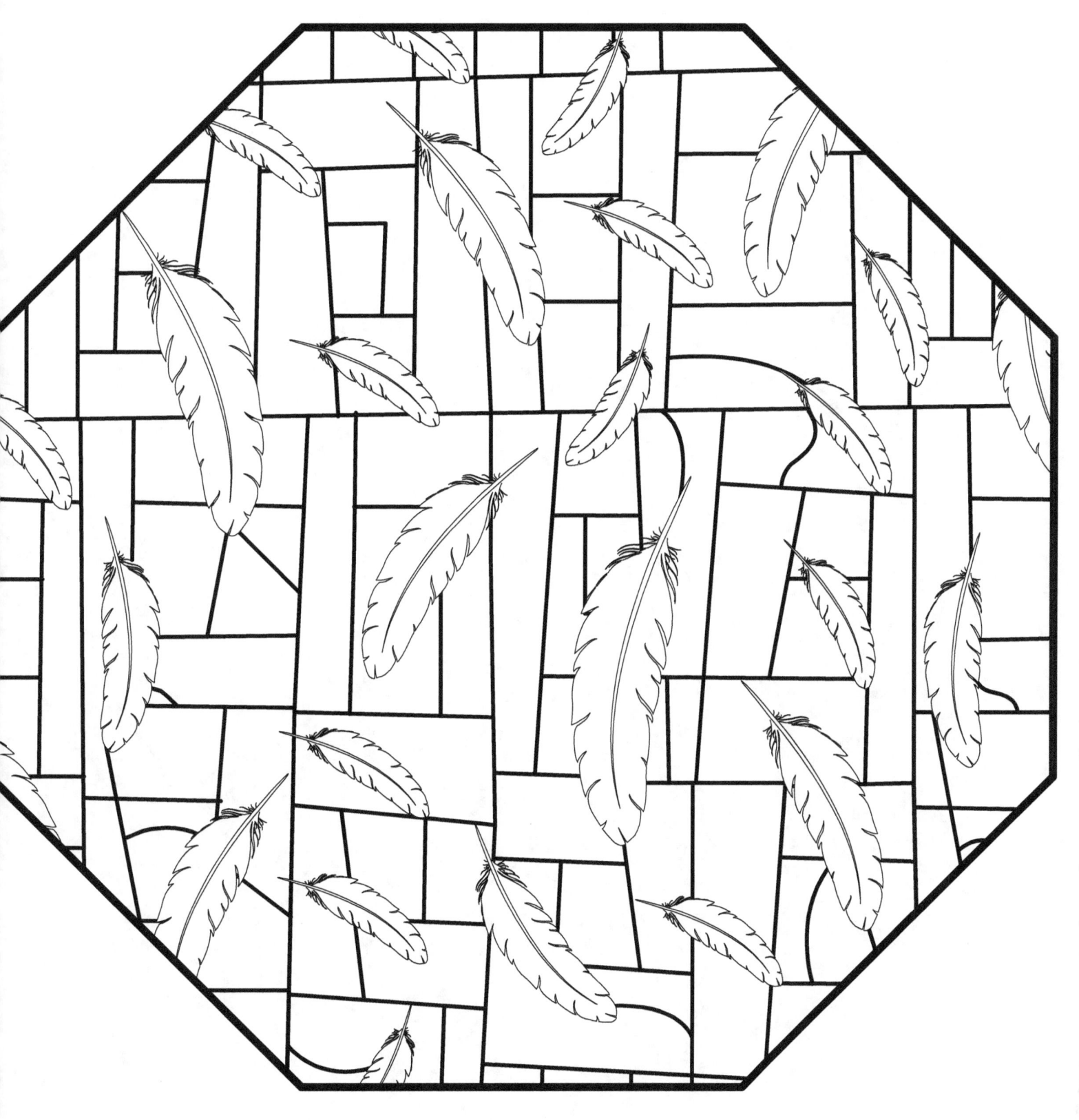

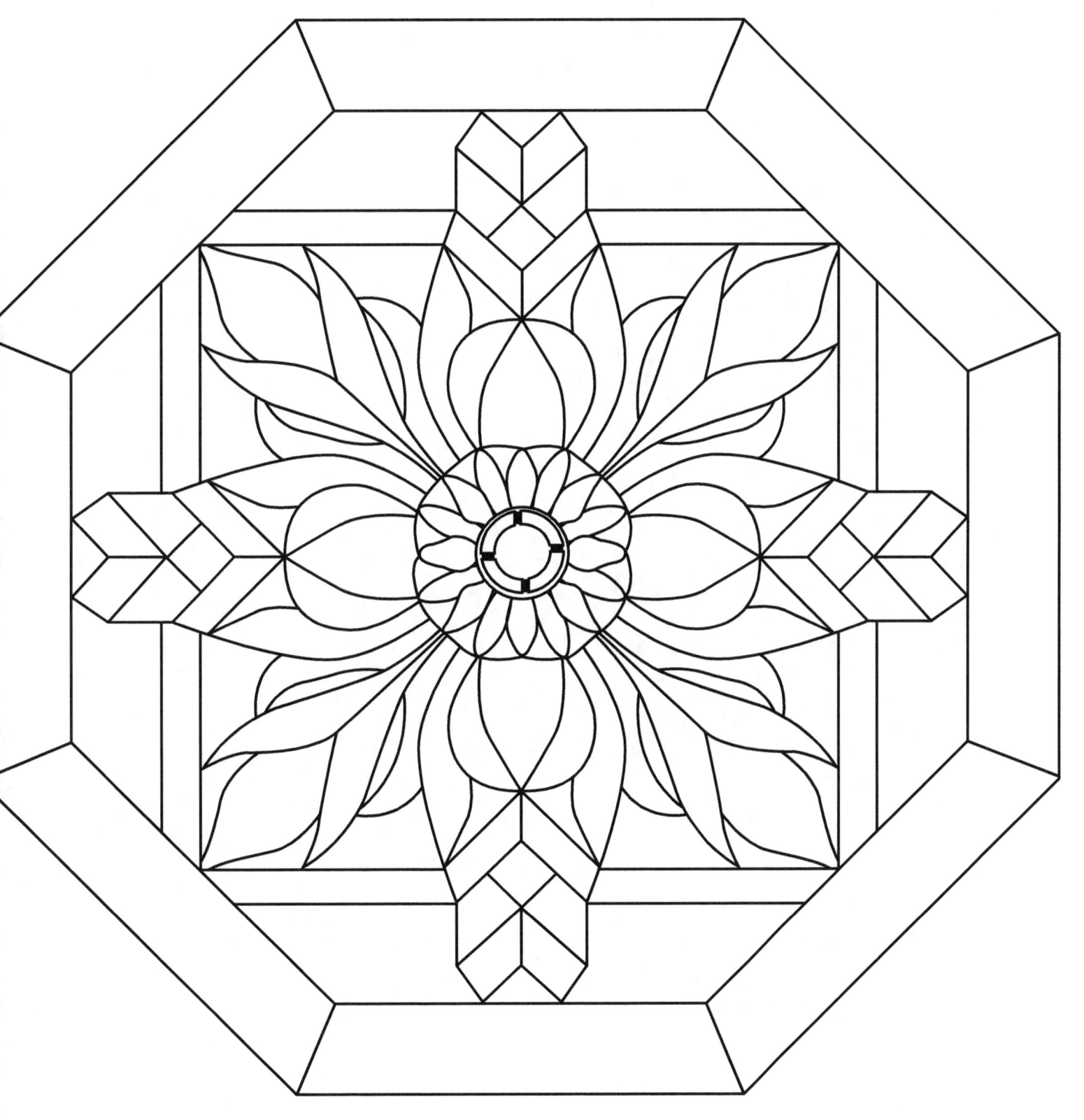

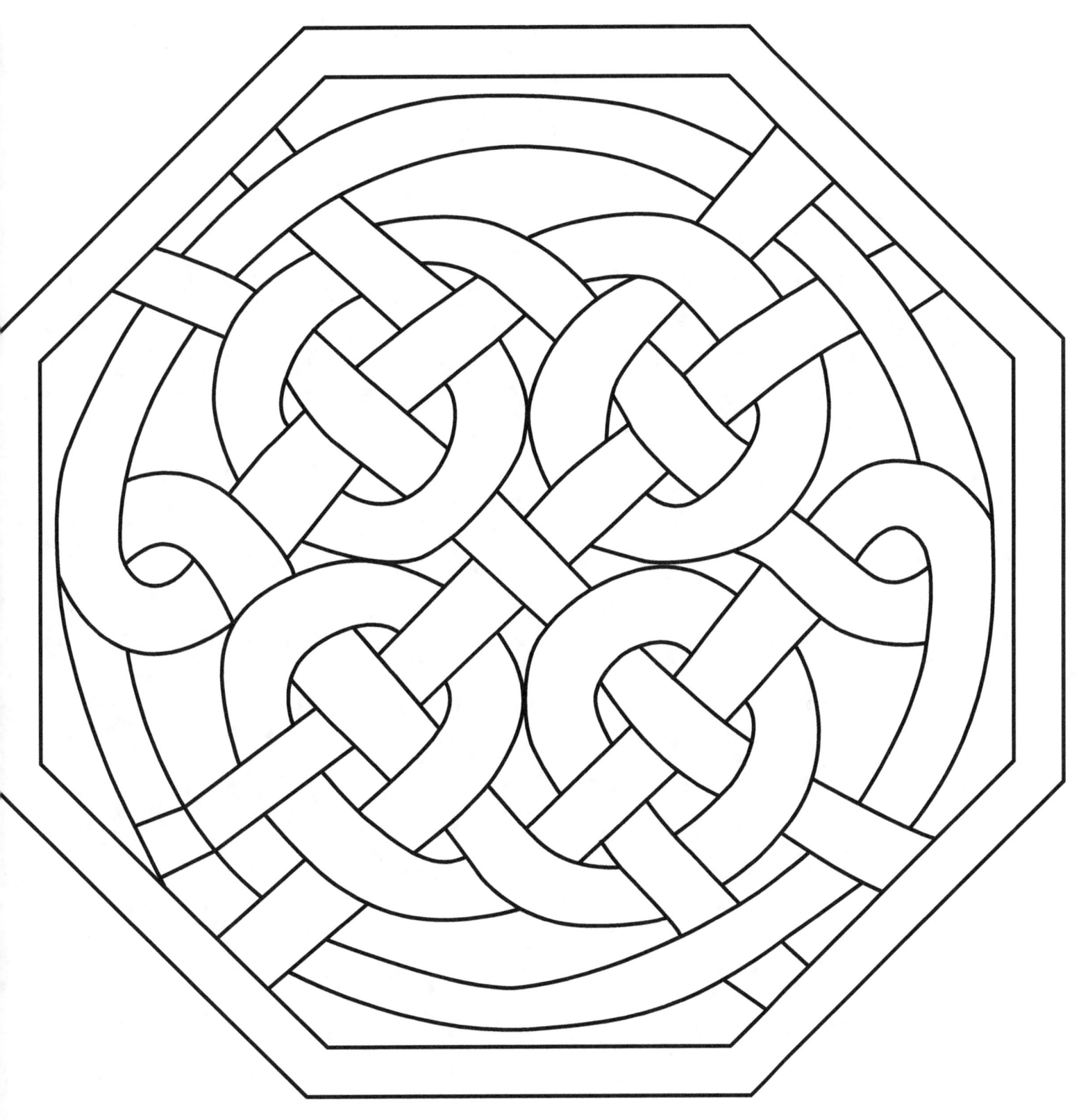

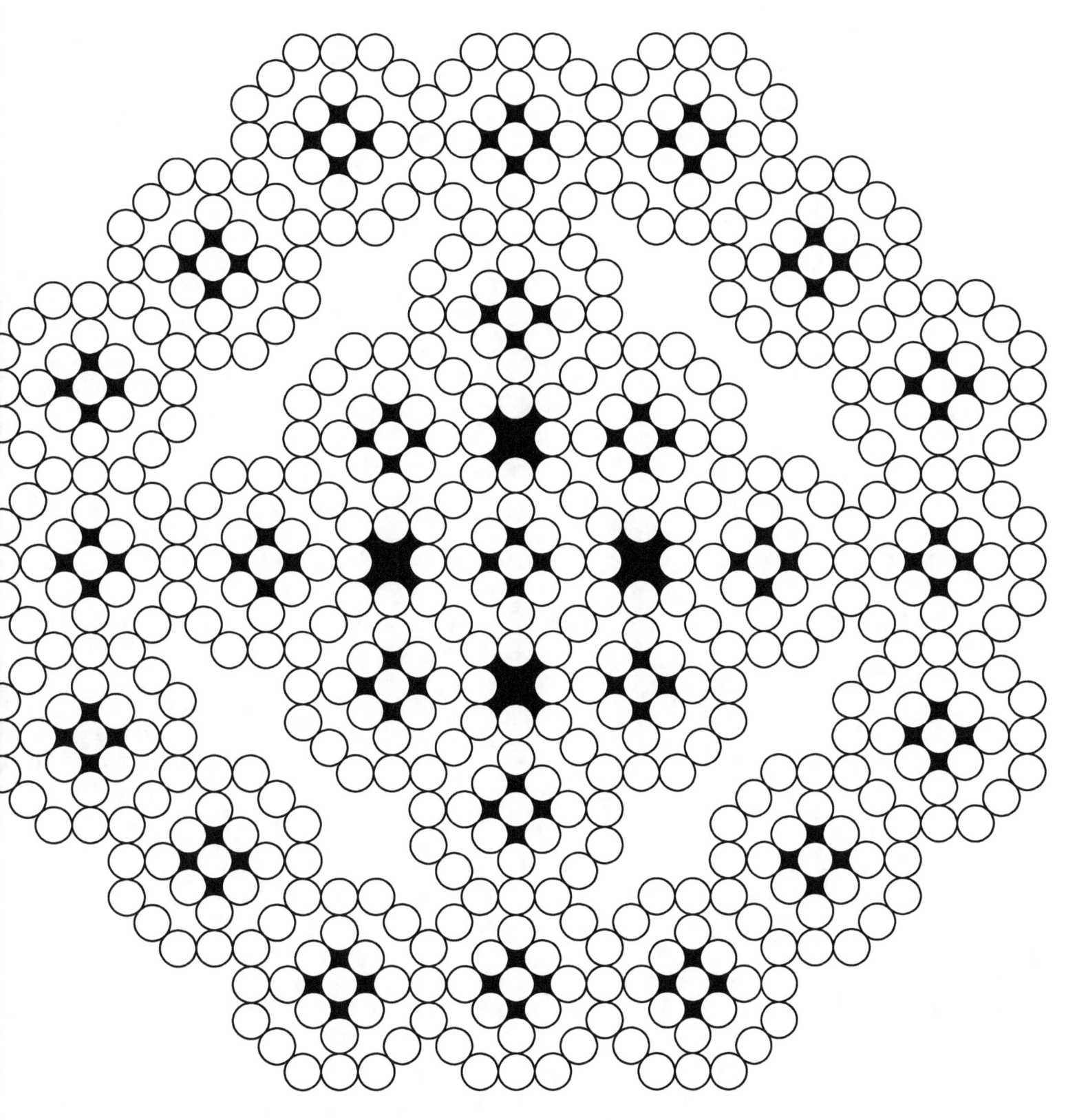

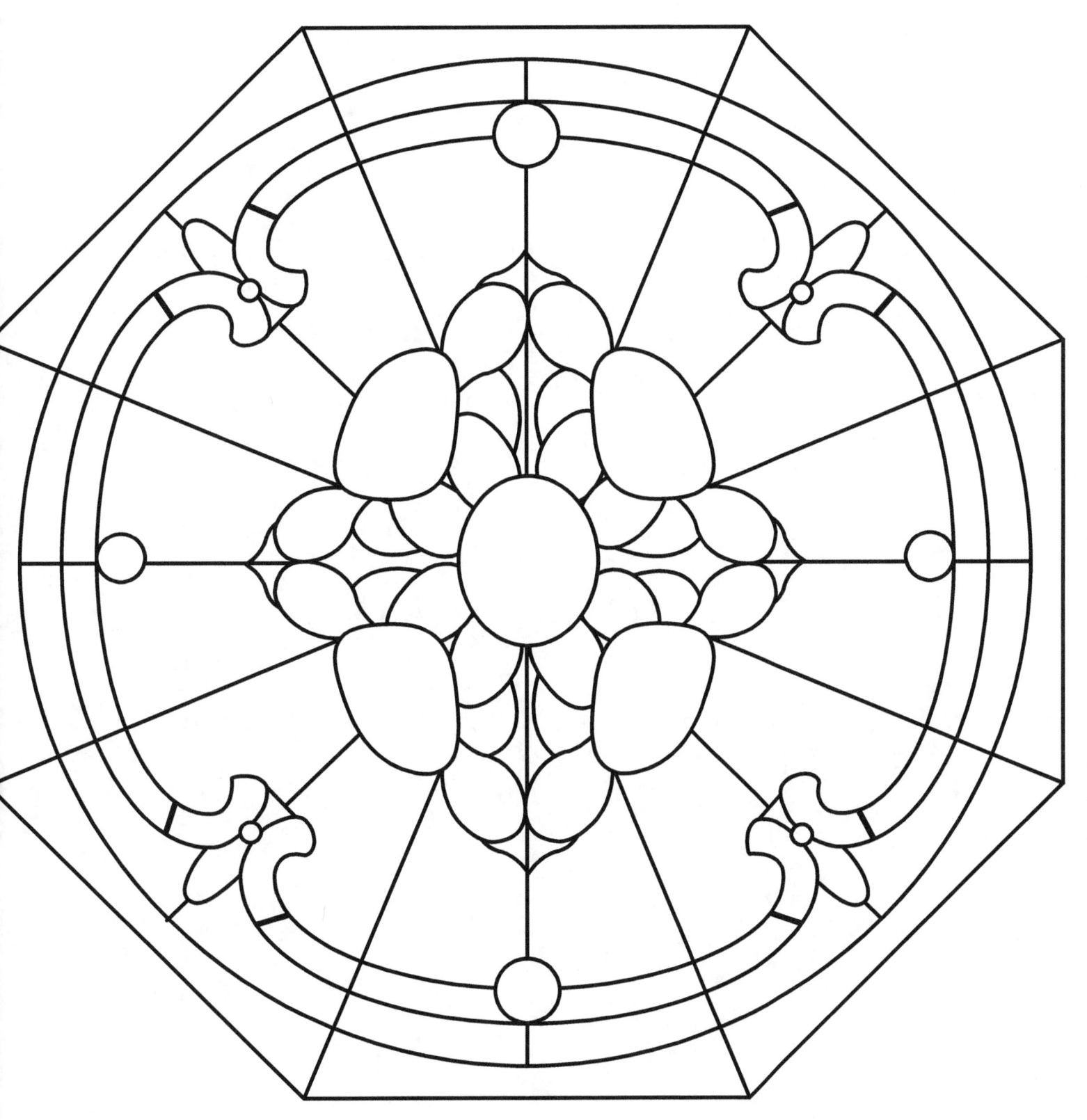

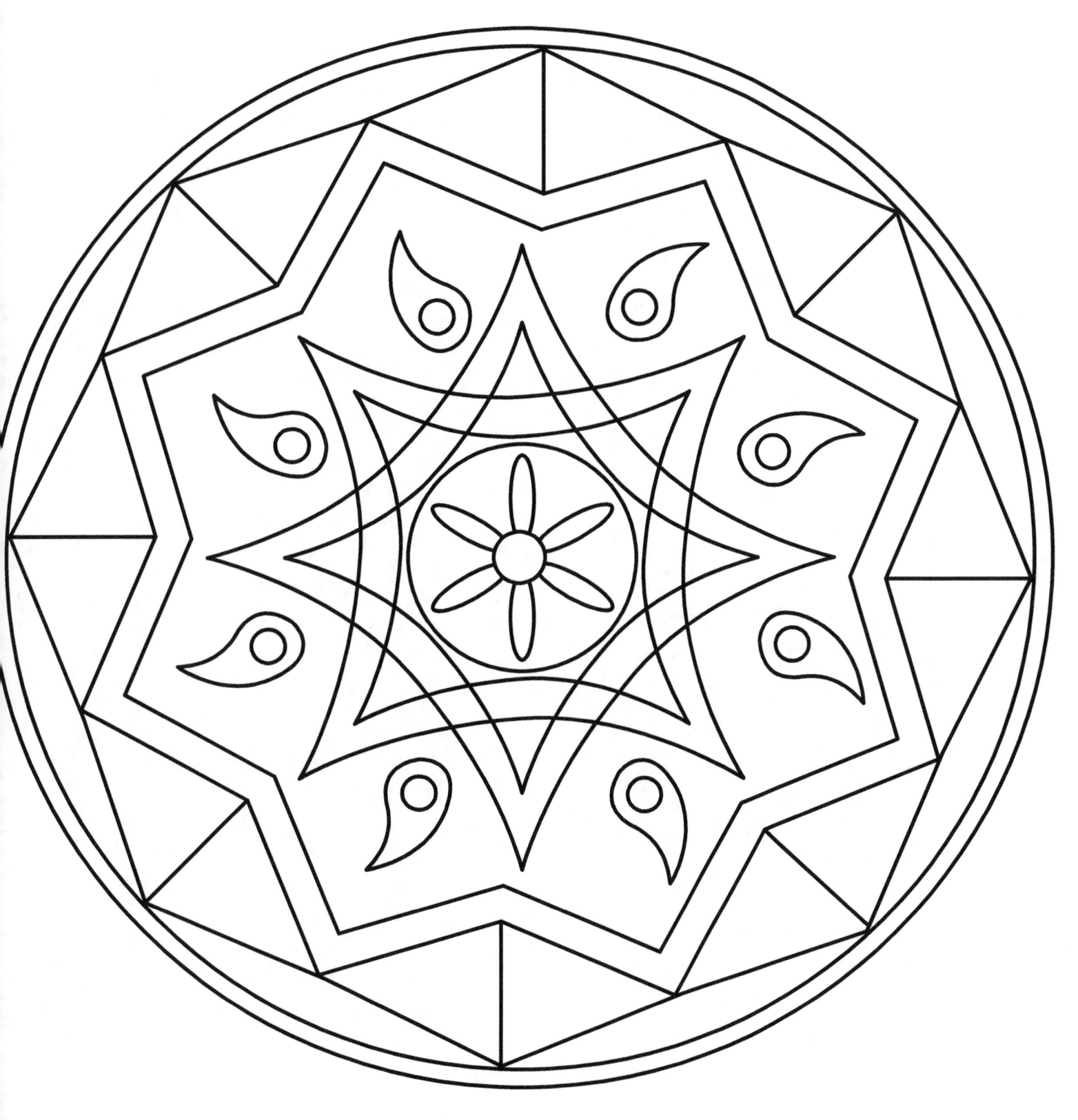

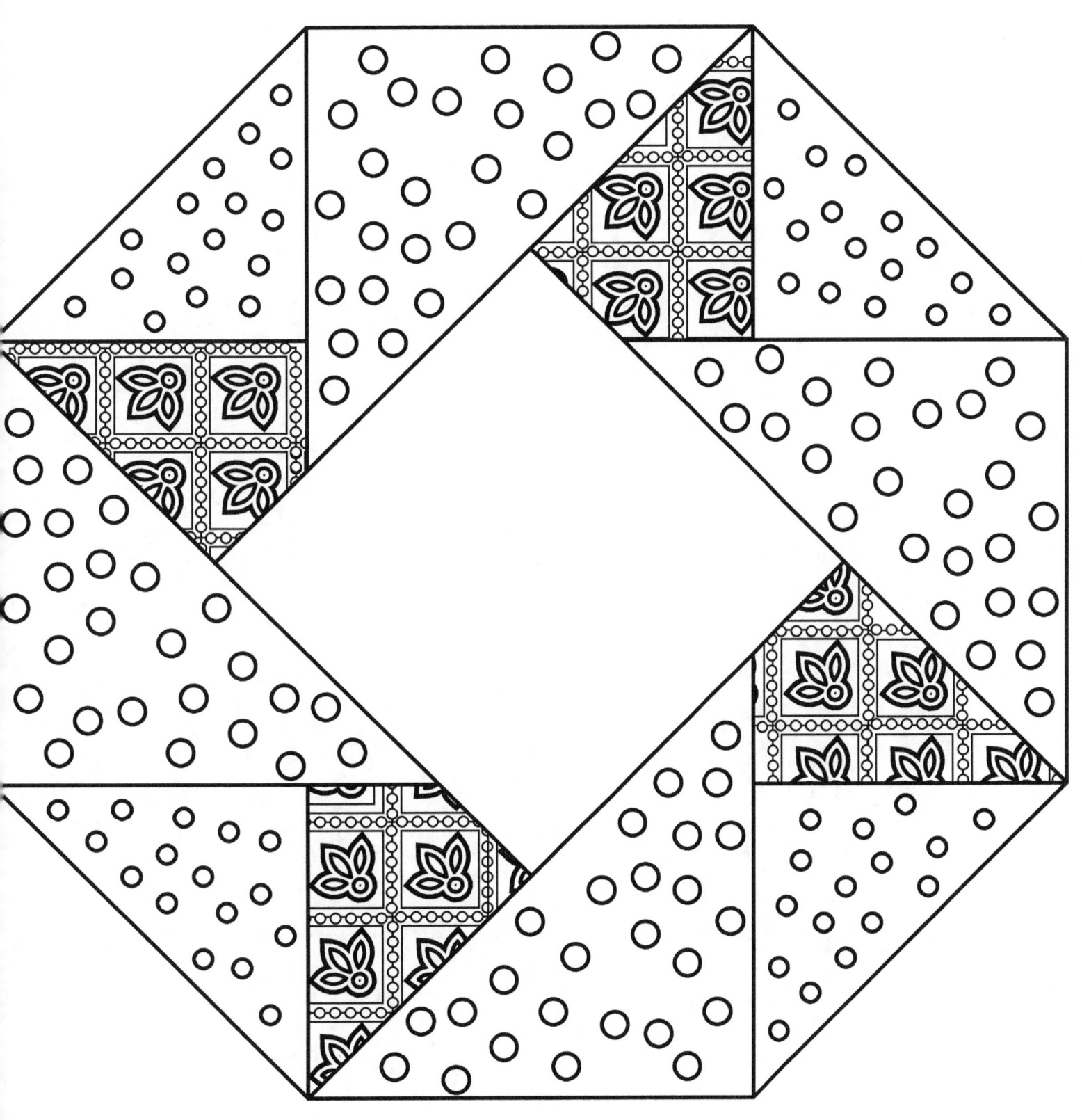

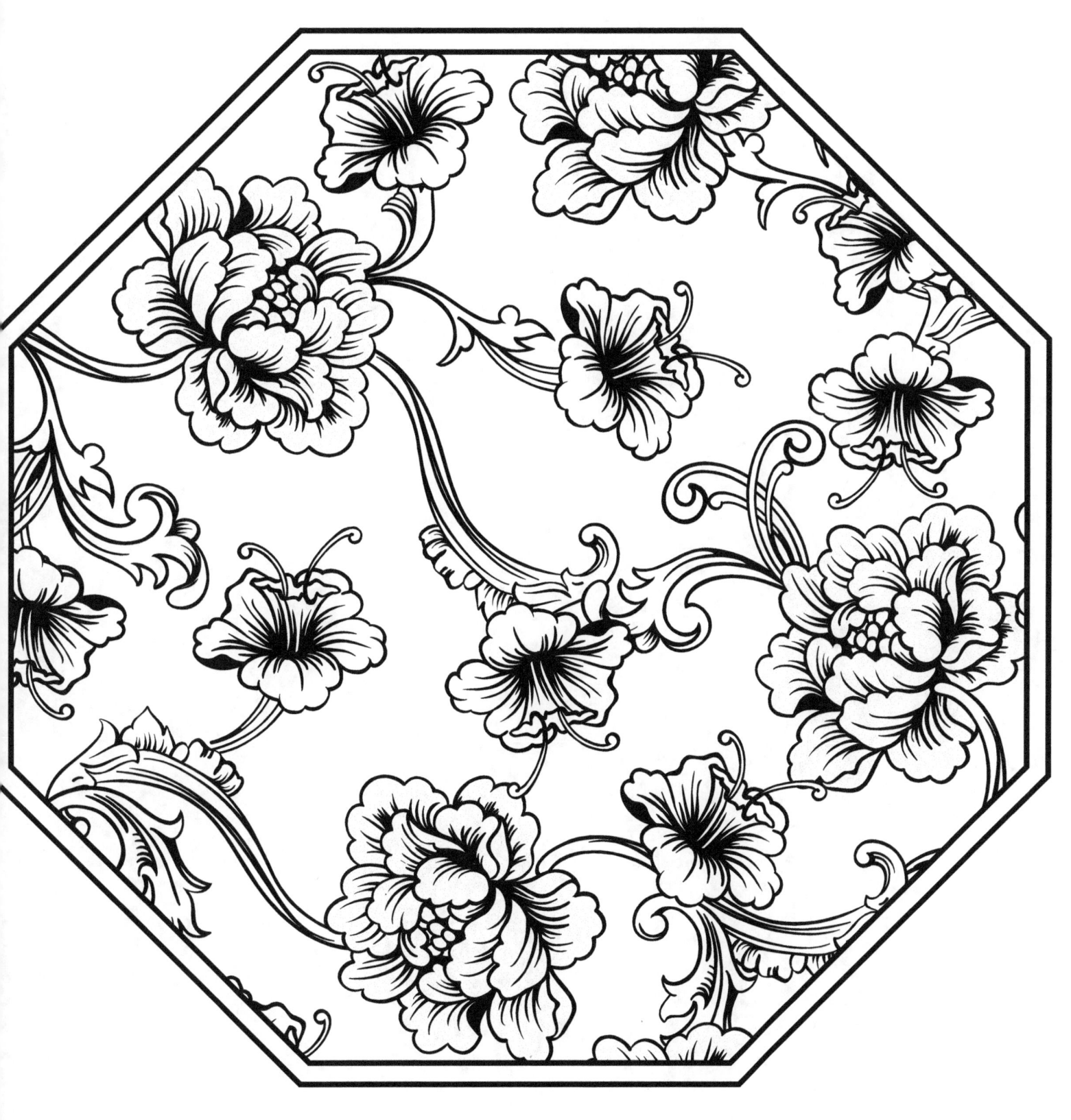

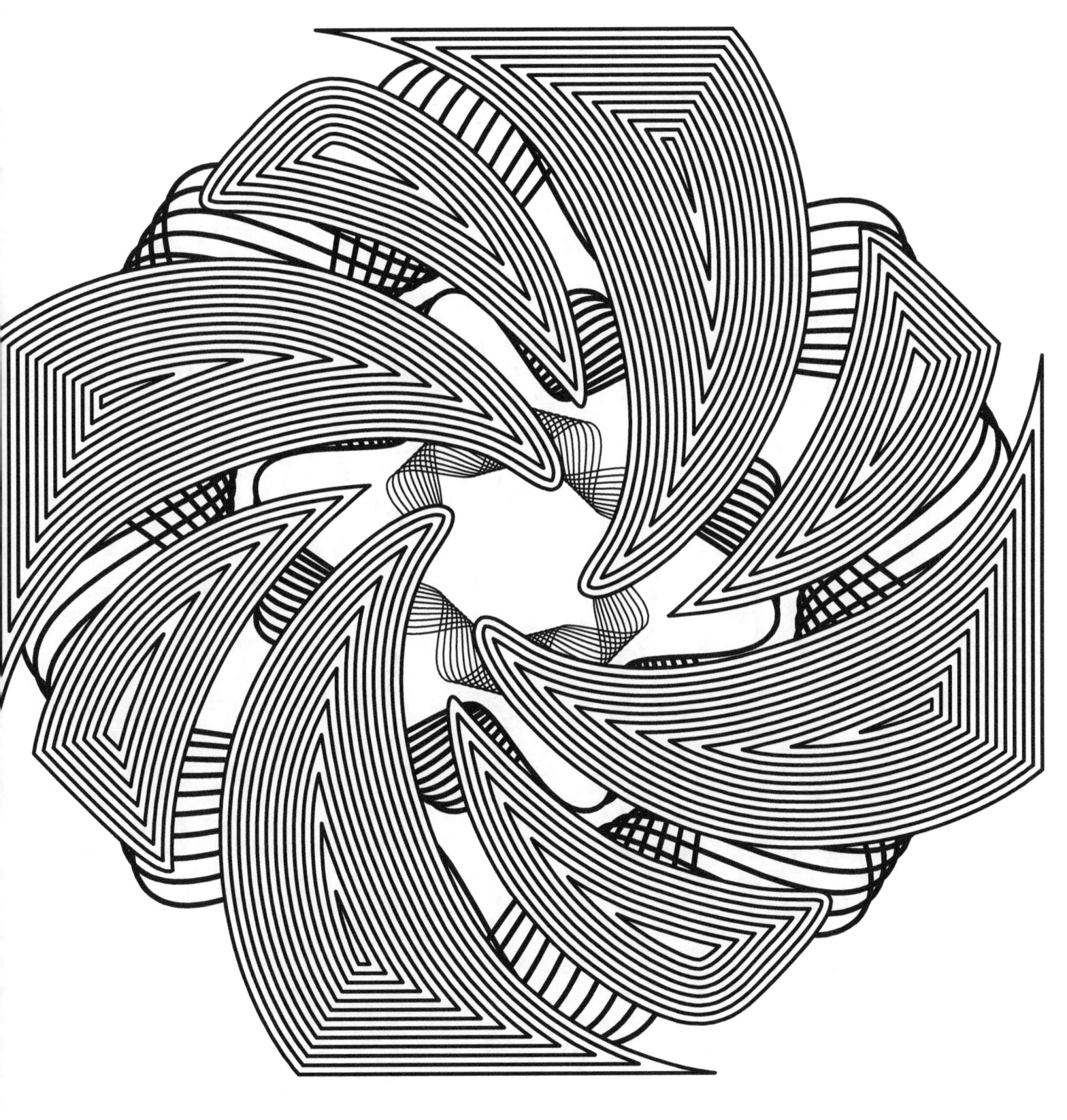

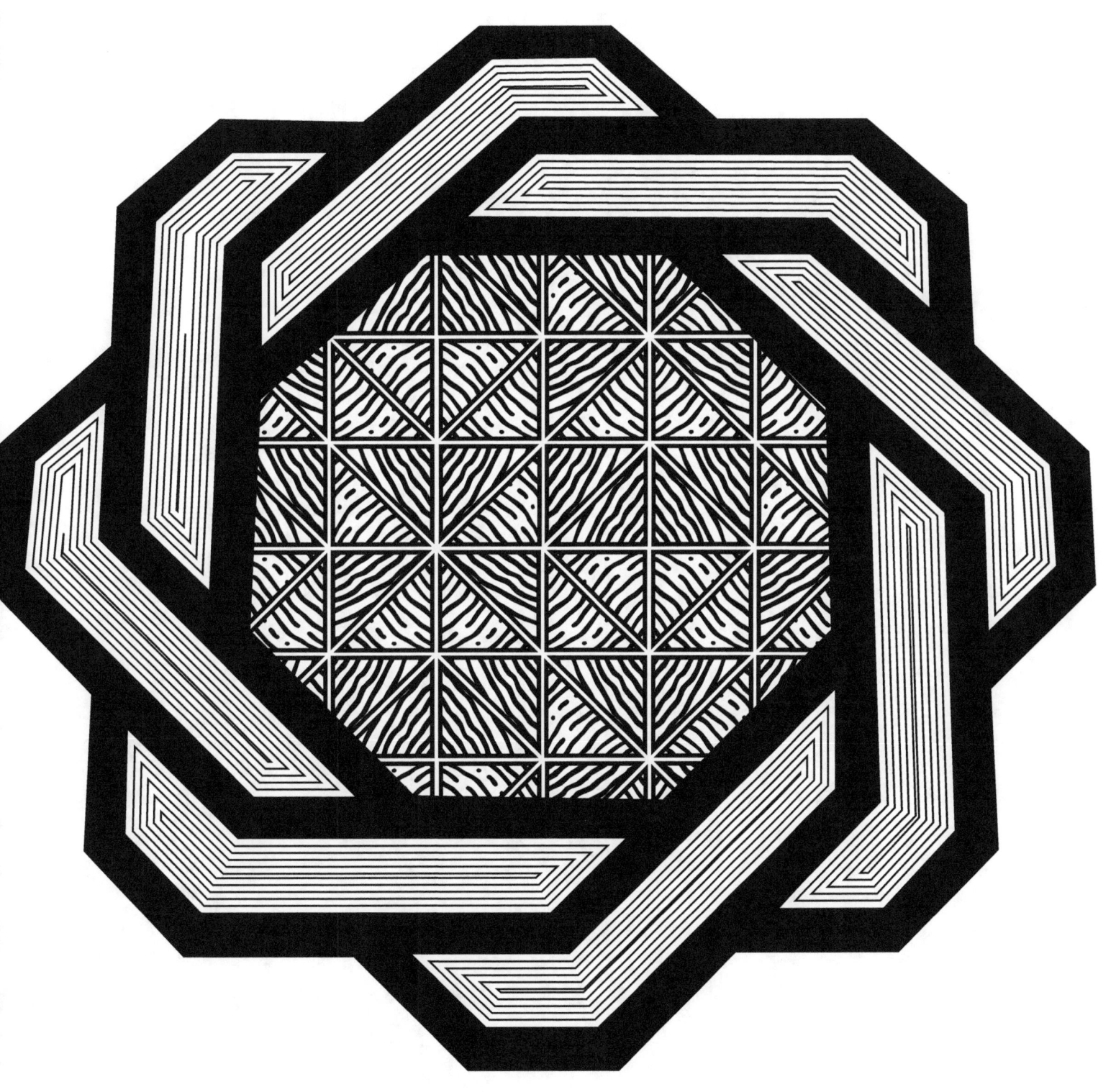

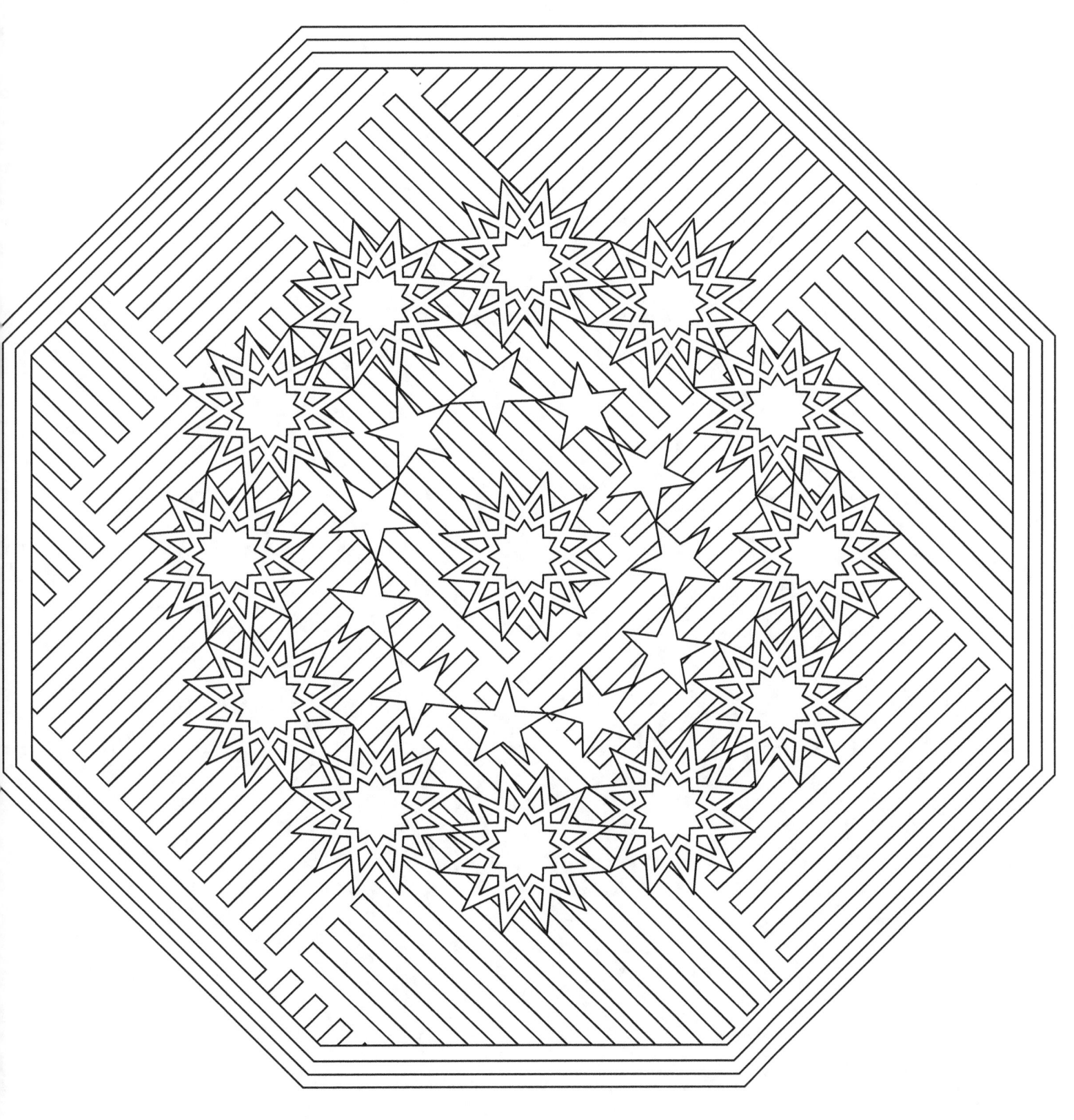

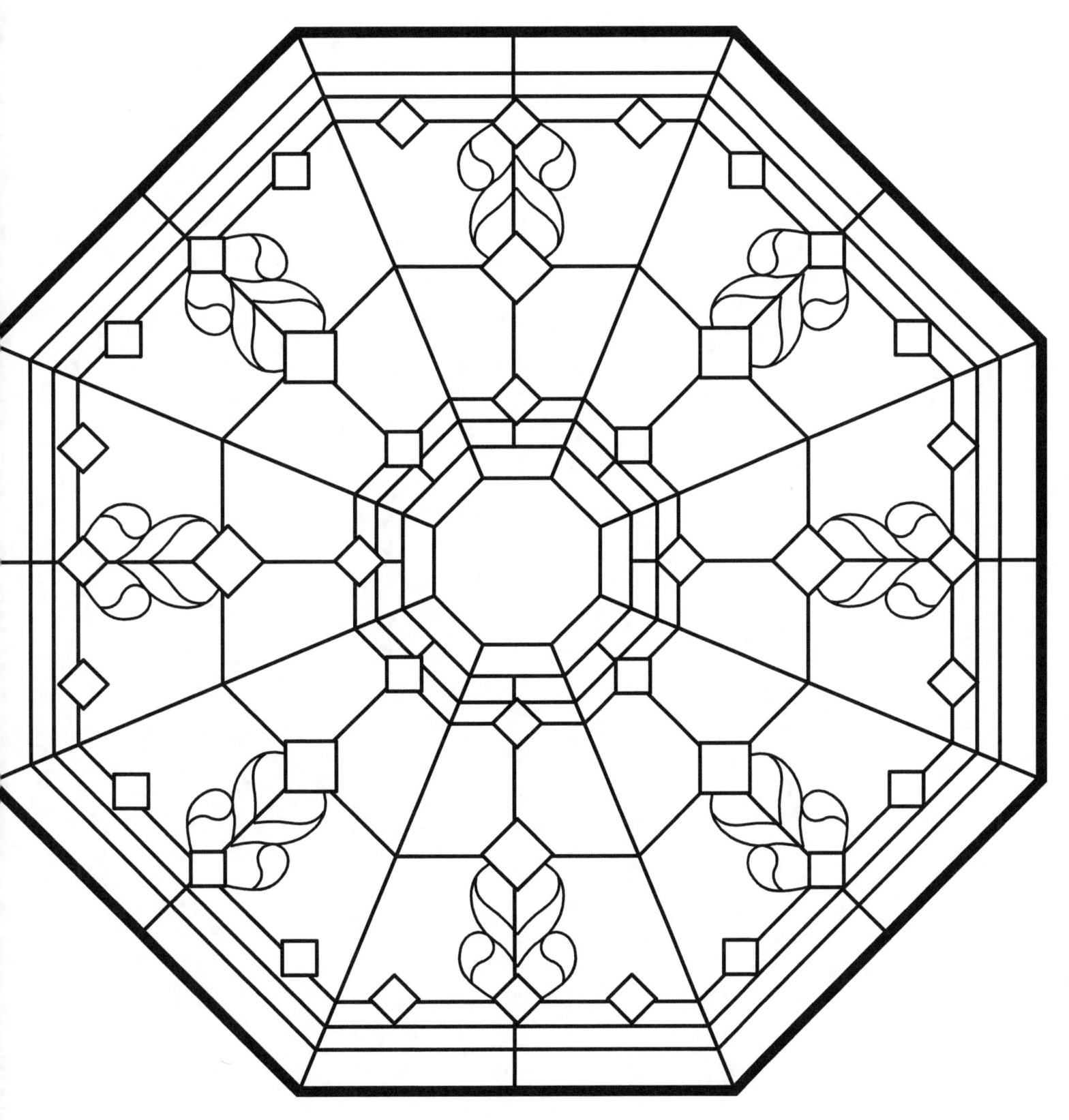

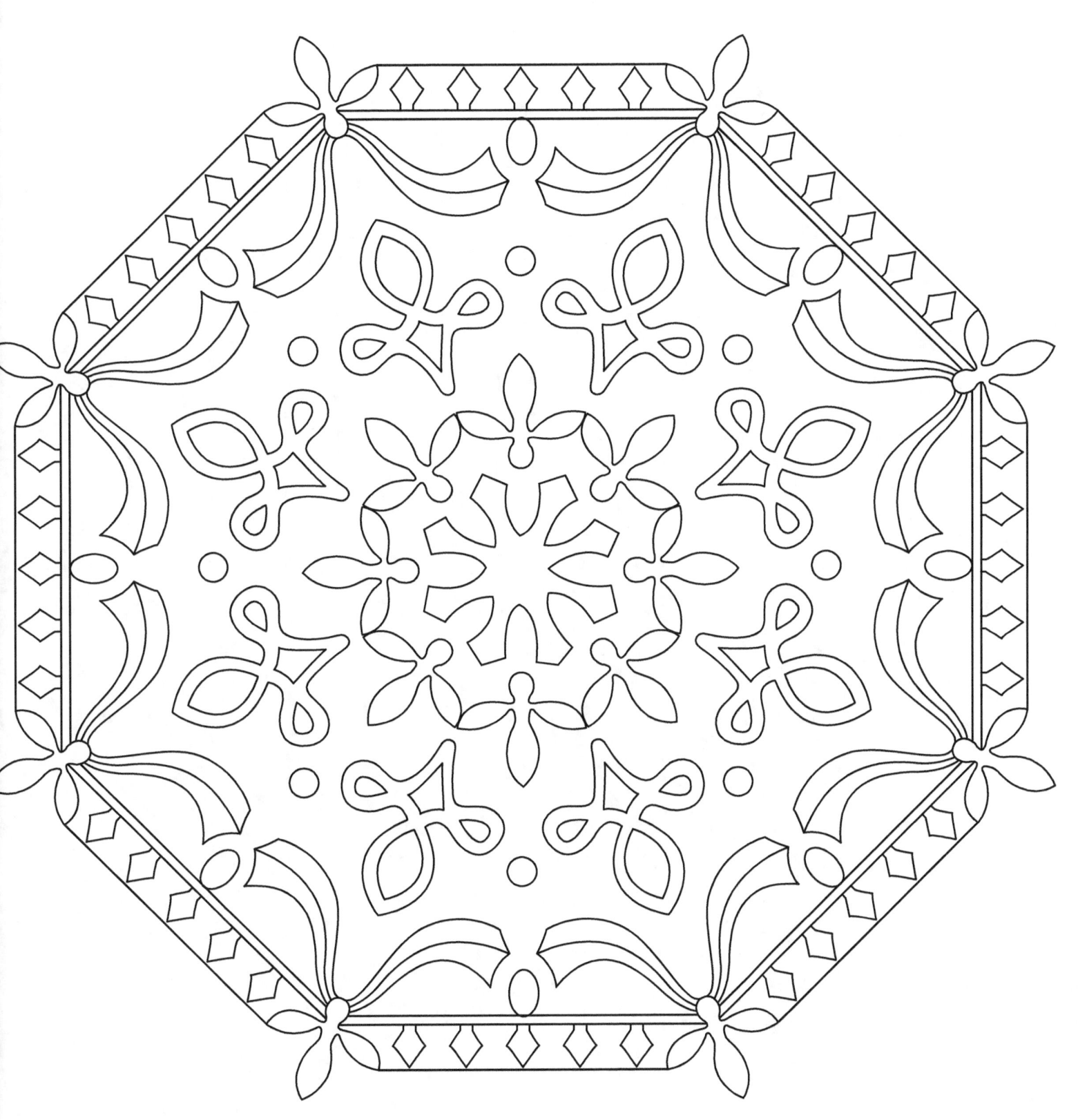

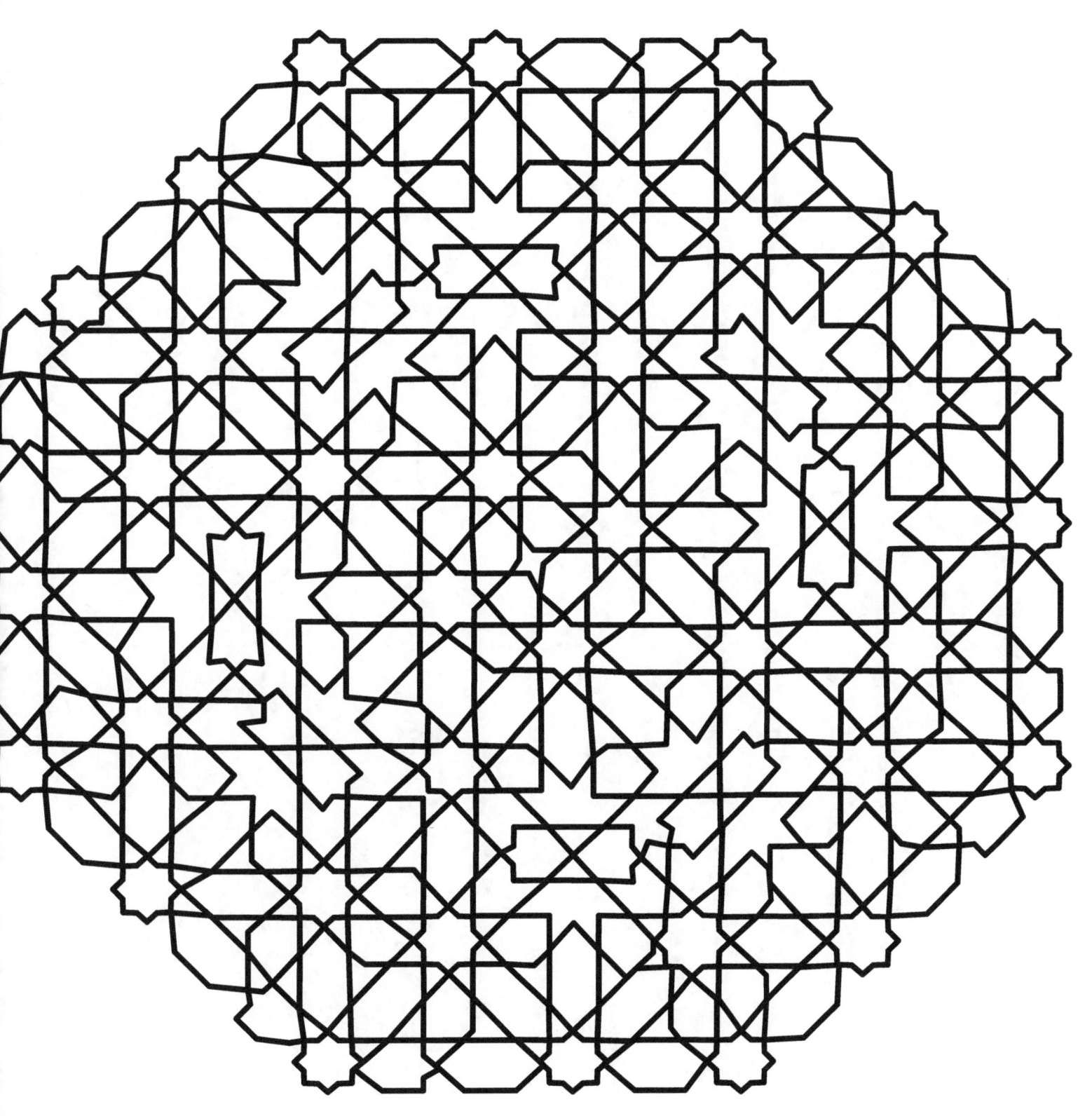

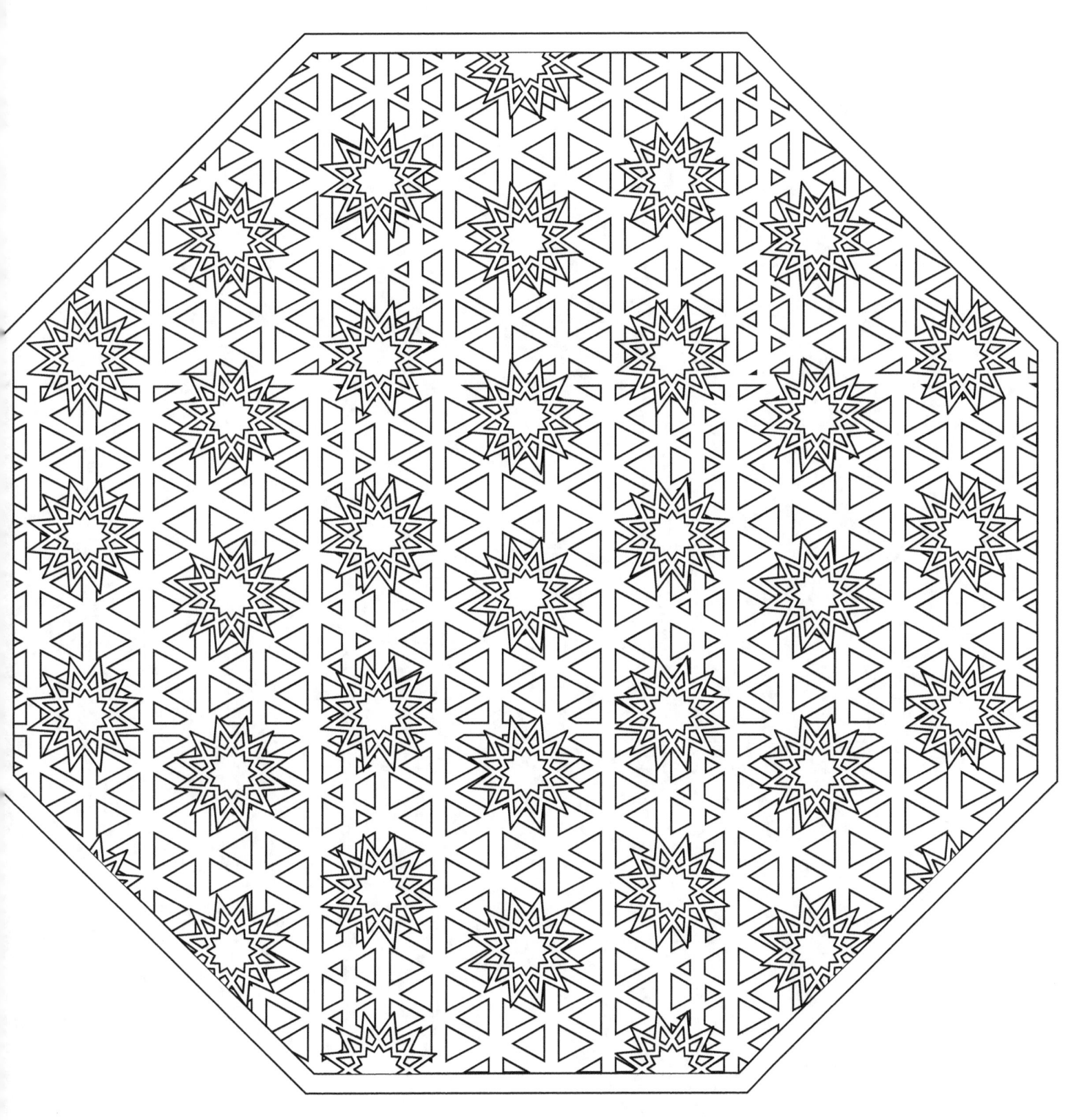

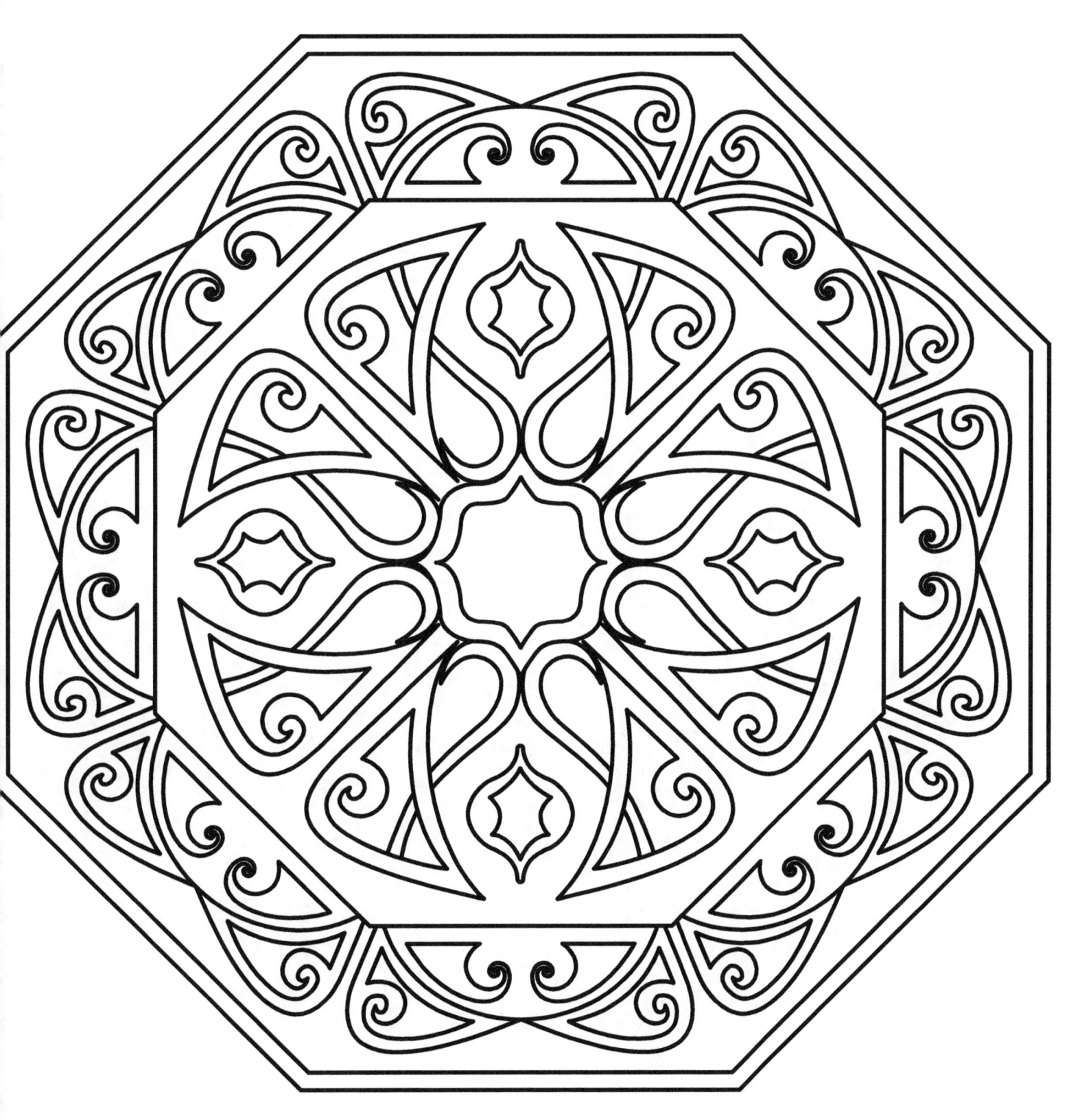

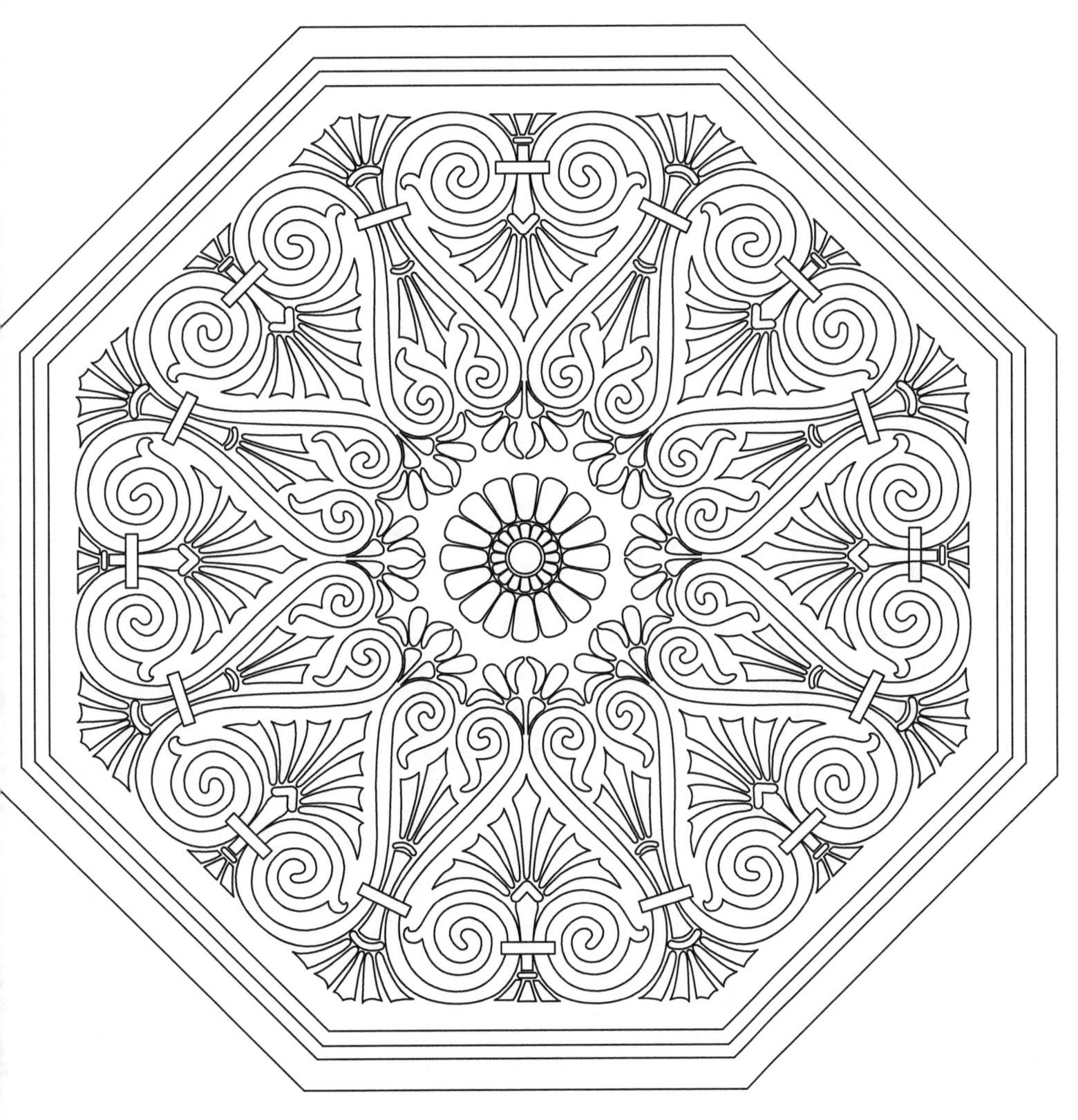

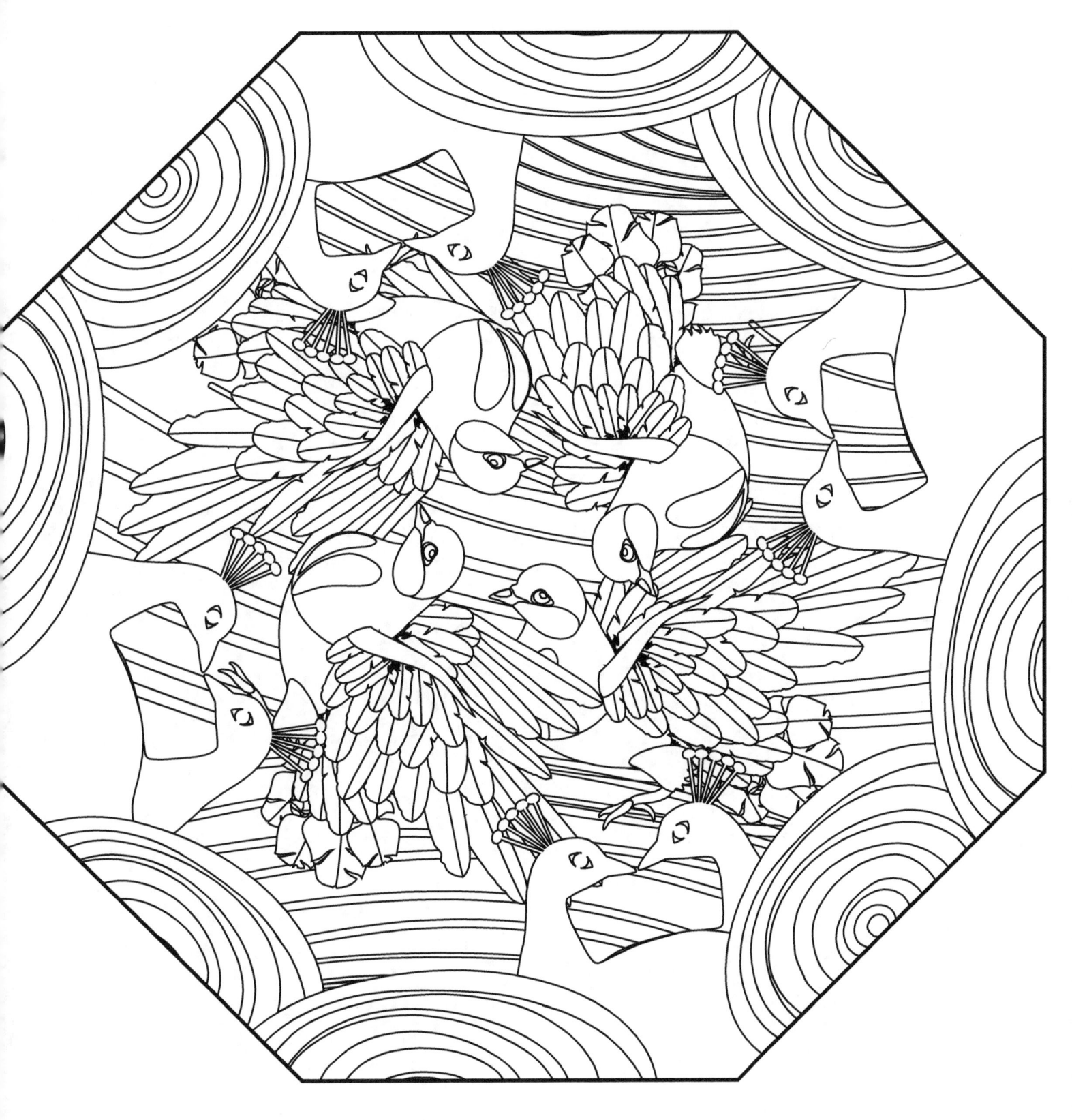

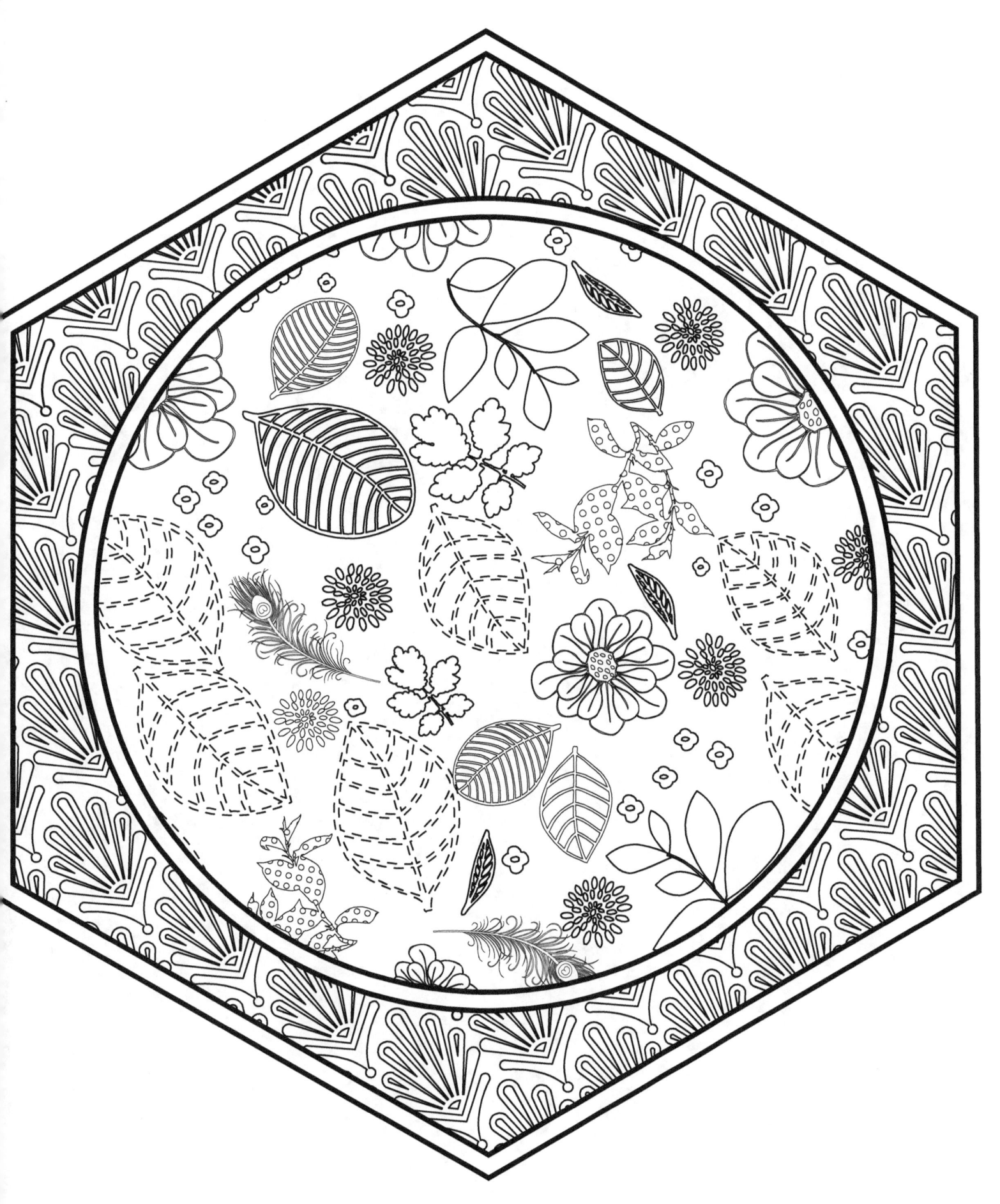

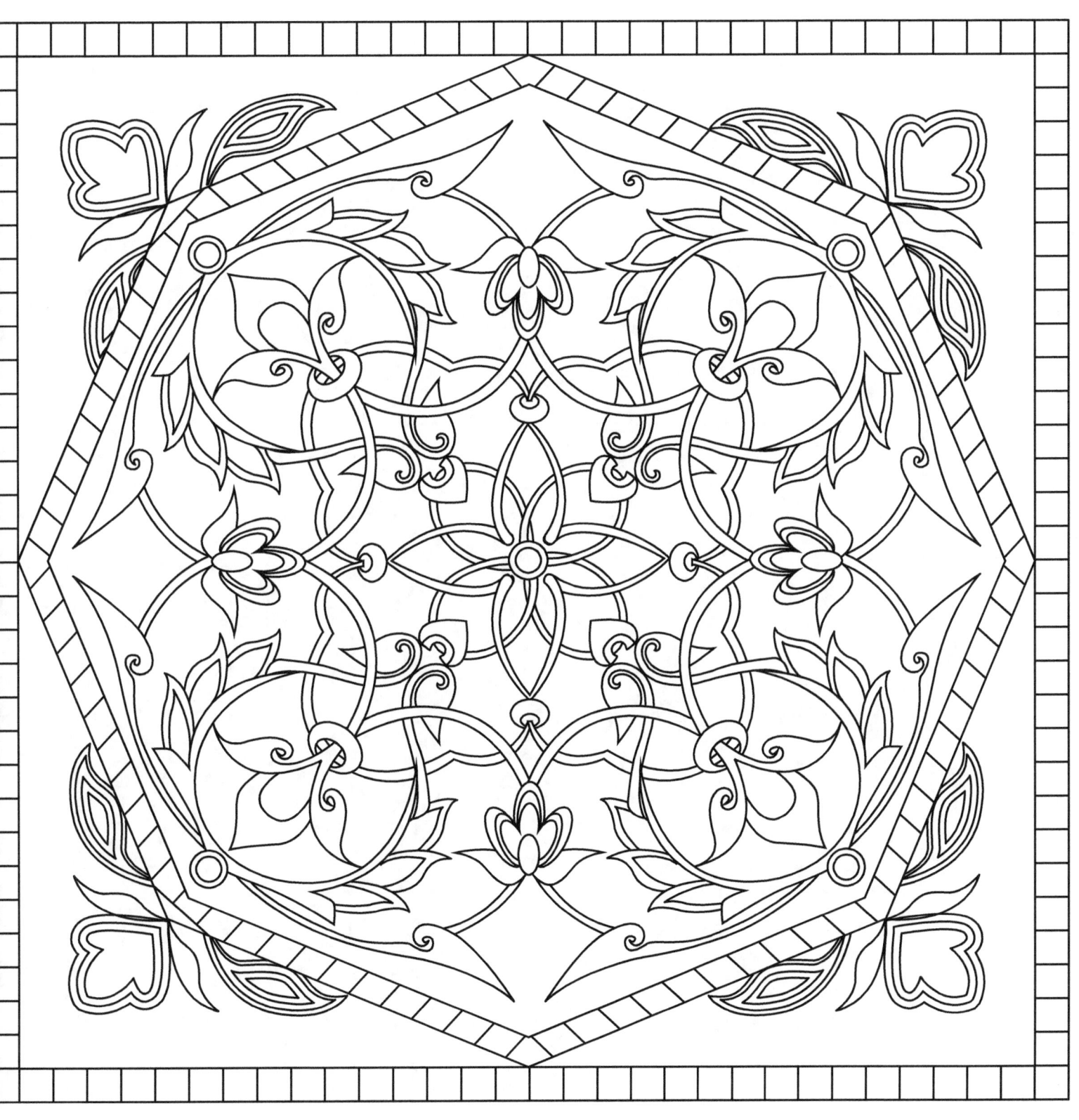

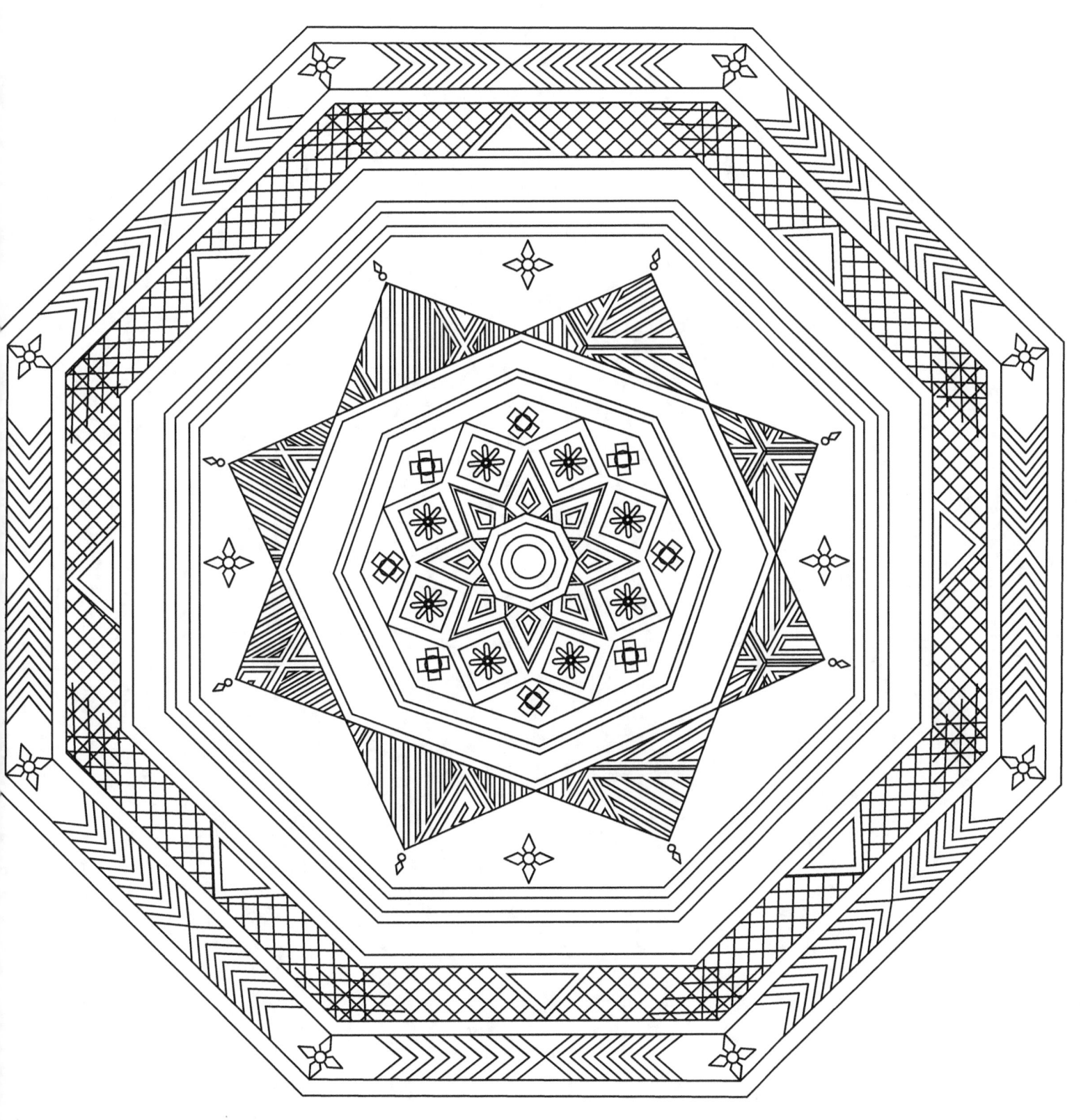

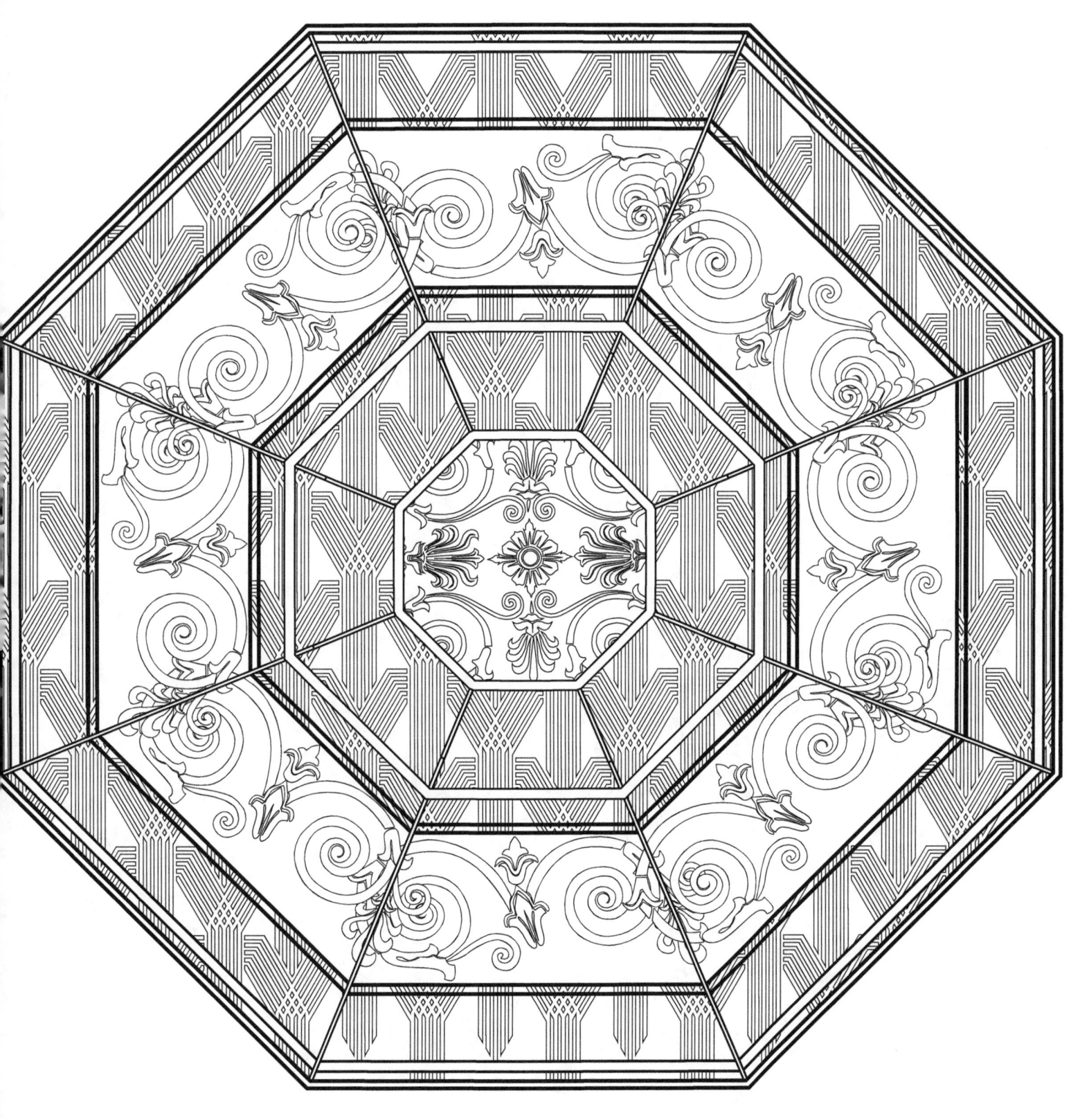

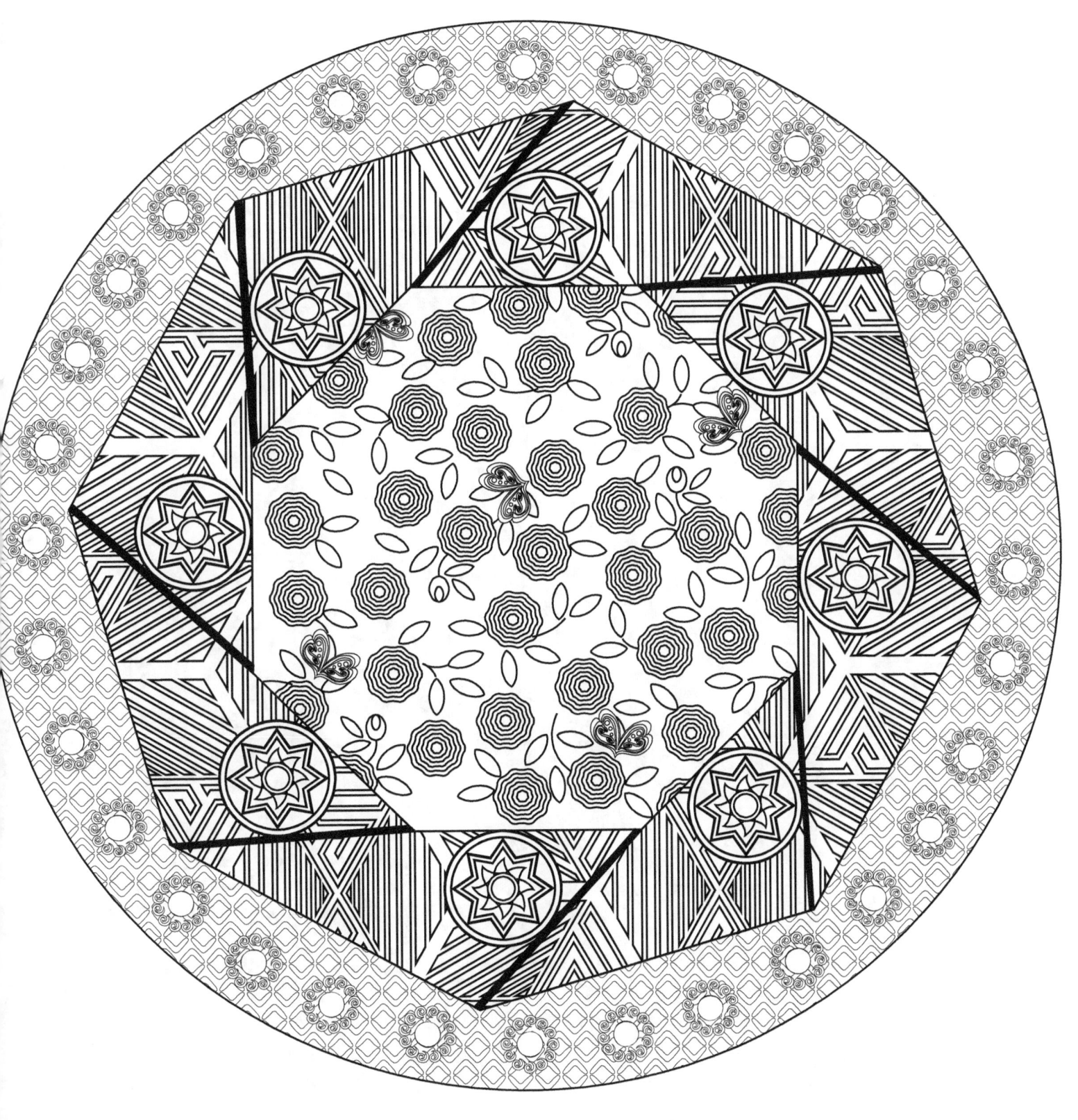